W9-CVA-334

SIDE by SIDE

THIRD EDITION

BOOK
1A

Steven J. Molinsky
Bill Bliss

Illustrated by

Richard E. Hill

Longman

Side by Side, 3rd edition
Student Book/Workbook 1A

Copyright © 2001 by Prentice Hall Regents
Addison Wesley Longman, Inc.
A Pearson Education Company.
All rights reserved.
No part of this publication may be reproduced,
stored in a retrieval system, or transmitted
in any form or by any means, electronic, mechanical,
photocopying, recording, or otherwise,
without the prior permission of the publisher.

Pearson Education, 10 Bank Street, White Plains, NY 10606

Vice president, director of publishing: *Allen Ascher*
Editorial manager: *Pam Fishman*
Vice president, director of design and production: *Rhea Banker*
Associate director of electronic production: *Aliza Greenblatt*
Production manager: *Ray Keating*
Director of manufacturing: *Patrice Fraccio*
Digital layout specialist: *Wendy Wolf*
Associate art director: *Elizabeth Carlson*
Interior design: *Elizabeth Carlson, Wendy Wolf*
Cover design: *Elizabeth Carlson*
Copyediting: *Janet Johnston*

Contributing *Side by Side* Gazette authors: *Laura English, Meredith Westfall*

Photo credits: p. 25, Walter Hodges/Corbis; p. 26, (*top, left*) Rhoda Sidney/Stock Boston, (*top, right*) Stuart Cohen/The Image Works, (*bottom, left*) Will & Deni McIntyre/Tony Stone Images, NY, (*bottom, right*) Ariel Skelley/The Stock Market; p. 54, (*top*) Spencer Grant/Liaison Agency, Inc., (*bottom*) Bachmann/The Image Works; p. 77, (*center*) Liane Enkelis/Stock Boston, (*left*) Bill Horsman/Stock Boston, (*right*) Robert Nickelsberg/Liaison Agency, Inc.; p. 78, (*top*) John Coletti/Stock Boston, (*second from top*) Torleif Svensson/The Stock Market, (*second from bottom*) Rick Smolan/Stock Boston, (*bottom*) Monika Graff/Stock Boston.

The authors gratefully acknowledge the contribution
of Tina Carver in the development of the original
Side by Side program.

ISBN 0-13-029298-2

3 4 5 6 7 8 9 10 – RRD – 05 04 03 02 01

CONTENTS

To Be: Introduction

- **Personal Information**
- **Meeting People**

VOCABULARY PREVIEW

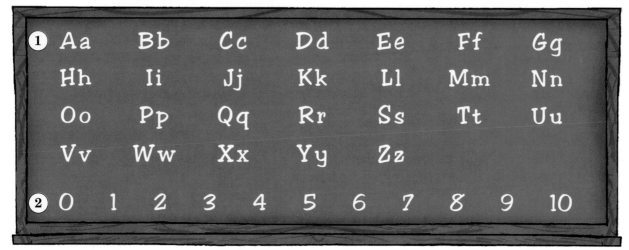

1. **Aa Bb Cc Dd Ee Ff Gg**
   Hh Ii Jj Kk Ll Mm Nn
   Oo Pp Qq Rr Ss Tt Uu
   Vv Ww Xx Yy Zz

2. **0 1 2 3 4 5 6 7 8 9 10**

1. alphabet   2. numbers

3. name   4. address   5. telephone number
phone number

What's Your Name?

* What's = What is
  235 = two thirty-five
  741-8906 = seven four one – eight nine "oh" six

Answer these questions.

1. What's your name?

   My name is Bruna.

2. What's your address?

   My address is Littlefield RD.

3. What's your phone number?

   My phone number is 530 2218.

4. Where are you from?

   I'm from Asunción Paraguay.

Now practice with other students in your class.

ROLE PLAY *A Famous Person*

Interview a famous person. Make up addresses, phone numbers, and cities. Use your imagination! Practice with another student. Then present your role play to the class.

A. What's your name?
B. My name is _Bruna Scott_.
A. _13135 Littlefield Rd_ address?
B. _Richmond VA._
A. _(804) 530 2218_ phone number?
B. _____.
A. Where are you from?
B. _I'm from Paraguay_.

a famous actor

a famous actress

a famous athlete

the president*
of your country

How to Say It!

Meeting People

A. Hello. My name is *Peter Lewis*.
B. Hi. I'm *Nancy Lee*. Nice to meet you.
A. Nice to meet you, too.

Practice conversations with other students.

* president / prime minister / leader

WHAT'S YOUR NAME?

My name is David Carter. I'm American. I'm from San Francisco.

My name is Mrs. Grant. My phone number is 549-2376.

My name is Ms. Martinez. My telephone number is (213) 694-5555. My fax number is (213) 694-5557.

My name is Peter Black. My address is 378 Main Street, Waterville, Florida. My license number is 921DCG.

My name is Susan Miller. My apartment number is 4-B.

My name is Mr. Santini. My e-mail address is TeacherJoe@worldnet.com.*

My name is William Chen. My address is 294 River Street, Brooklyn, New York. My telephone number is 469-7750. My social security number is 044-35-9862.

* "TeacherJoe at worldnet-dot-com"

✔ READING CHECK-UP

MATCH

___ 1. name   a. 549-2376

___ 2. address   b. 4-B

___ 3. phone number   c. TeacherJoe@worldnet.com

___ 4. apartment number   d. William Chen

___ 5. social security number   e. 378 Main Street

___ 6. e-mail address   f. 044-35-9862

LISTENING

Listen and choose the correct answer.

1. a. Mary Black
    b. Mrs. Grant
2. a. 265 River Street
    b. 265 Main Street
3. a. 5-C
    b. 9-D

4. a. 295-4870
    b. 259-4087
5. a. 032-98-6175
    b. 032-89-6179
6. a. maryb@worldnet.com
    b. garyd@worldnet.com

INTERVIEW *Spelling Names*

Practice the conversation.

A. What's your last name?
B. *Kelly.*
A. How do you spell that?
B. *K-E-L-L-Y.*
A. What's your first name?
B. *Sarah.*
A. How do you spell that?
B. *S-A-R-A-H.*

Now interview students in your class.

	LAST NAME	FIRST NAME
1.		
2.		
3.		
4.		
5.		
6.		
7.		
8.		

PRONUNCIATION *Linked Sounds*

Listen. Then say it.

My name is Maria.

My address is 10 Main Street.

My apartment number is 3B.

Say it. Then listen.

My name is David.

My address is 9 River Street.

My phone number is 941-2238.

SIDE by SIDE JOURNAL

Write about yourself in your journal.

My name is ___Bruno___.

My address is ___13135 Little Field Rd___.

My phone number is ___804- 530 22 18___.

I'm from _____.

CHAPTER SUMMARY

GRAMMAR

To Be

am	I am from Mexico City. (I am)
is	What's your name? (What is) My name is Maria.
are	Where are you from?

KEY VOCABULARY

PERSONAL INFORMATION

name
first name
last name
address
e-mail address

telephone number
phone number
apartment number
fax number

MEETING PEOPLE

Hello.
Hi.

My name is _____.
I'm _____.
Nice to meet you.
 Nice to meet you, too.

To Be + Location
Subject Pronouns

- **Classroom Objects**
- **Rooms in the Home**
- **Cities and Nationalities**
- **Places Around Town**

VOCABULARY PREVIEW

1. pen	6. bank	11. living room
2. pencil	7. supermarket	12. dining room
3. book	8. post office	13. kitchen
4. desk	9. restaurant	14. bedroom
5. computer	10. library	15. bathroom

In the Classroom

1. pen	**6.** globe	**10.** clock	**14.** chair
2. book	**7.** map	**11.** bulletin board	**15.** ruler
3. pencil	**8.** board	**12.** computer	**16.** desk
4. notebook	**9.** wall	**13.** table	**17.** dictionary
5. bookshelf			

Where Is It?

(Where is) Where's the book?	(It is) It's on the desk.

Where's the book?

It's on the desk.

Where's the map?

It's on the wall.

Where's the computer?

It's on the table.

1. Where's the pen?

2. Where's the board?

3. Where's the globe?

4. Where's the ruler?

5. Where's the pencil?

6. Where's the clock?

7. Where's the notebook?

8. Where's the dictionary?

9. Where's the bulletin board?

Make a List!

Work with another student. Make a list of all the objects in your classroom. Present your list to the class. Who has the best list?

9

1. living room
2. dining room
3. kitchen

4. bedroom
5. bathroom
6. attic

7. yard
8. garage
9. basement

Where Are You?

Where	am	I		?
	is	he / she / it		
	are	we / you / they		

(I am)	I'm	
(He is)	He's	
(She is)	She's	
(It is)	It's	in the kitchen.
(We are)	We're	
(You are)	You're	
(They are)	They're	

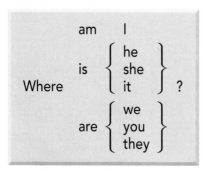

Where are you? — I'm in the kitchen.

Where are you? — We're in the living room.

Where are Mr. and Mrs. Jones? — They're in the yard.

1. Where are you?

2. Where are you?

3. Where are Jim and Pam?

4. Where are you?

5. Where are Mr. and Mrs. Park?

6. Where are you?

7. Where are you?

8. Where are you and Ben?

9. Where are Mr. and Mrs. Hernandez?

Where's Bob?

* Where's = Where is

1. Where's Tim?

2. Where's Rosa?

3. Where's the newspaper?

4. Where's Peggy?

5. Where's the telephone book?

6. Where's Harry?

7. Where's Ellen?

8. Where's Kevin?

9. Where's the cell phone?

READING

THE STUDENTS IN MY ENGLISH CLASS

The students in my English class are very interesting. Henry is Chinese. He's from Shanghai. Linda is Puerto Rican. She's from San Juan. Mr. and Mrs. Kim are Korean. They're from Seoul.

George is Greek. He's from Athens. Carla is Italian. She's from Rome. Mr. and Mrs. Sato are Japanese. They're from Tokyo. My friend Maria and I are Mexican. We're from Mexico City.

Yes, the students in my English class are very interesting. We're from many different countries . . . and we're friends.

✔ READING CHECK-UP

TRUE OR FALSE?

___ 1. Linda is Korean.

___ 2. George is Greek.

___ 3. Henry is from Mexico City.

___ 4. Mr. Kim is from Seoul.

___ 5. Carla is Chinese.

___ 6. The students in the class are from many countries.

How About You?

Tell about the students in YOUR English class. Where are they from?

How to Say It!

Greeting People

A. Hi. How are you?
B. Fine. And you?
A. Fine, thanks.

Practice conversations with other students.

Where Are They?

Ask and answer questions based on these pictures.

1. _____ Albert?

_____ .

2. _____ Carmen?

_____ .

3. _____ Walter and Mary?

_____ .

4. _____ you?

_____ .

5. _____ you?

_____ .

6. _____ Kate?

_____ .

7. _____ Mr. and Mrs. Lee?

_____ .

8. _____ monkey?

_____ .

9. _____ I?

_____ .

Now add people and places of your own.

10. _____ ?

_____ .

11. _____ ?

_____ .

12. _____ ?

_____ .

READING

George

Maria

SOCIAL SECURITY

Mr. and Mrs. Sato

our English teacher

ALL THE STUDENTS IN MY ENGLISH CLASS ARE ABSENT TODAY

All the students in my English class are absent today. George is absent. He's in the hospital. Maria is absent. She's at the dentist. Mr. and Mrs. Sato are absent. They're at the social security office. Even our English teacher is absent. He's home in bed!

What a shame! Everybody in my English class is absent today. Everybody except me.

 READING *CHECK-UP*

WHAT'S THE ANSWER?

1. Where's George?
2. Where's Maria?
3. Where are Mr. and Mrs. Sato?
4. Where's the English teacher?

How About You?

Tell about YOUR English class:
Which students are in class today?
Which students are absent today?
Where are they?

LISTENING

WHAT'S THE WORD?

Listen and choose the correct answer.

1. a. bank
   b. park
2. a. hospital
   b. library
3. a. He's
   b. She's
4. a. He's
   b. She's
5. a. We're
   b. They're
6. a. We're
   b. They're

WHERE ARE THEY?

Listen and choose the correct place.

1. a. living room
   b. dining room
2. a. bathroom
   b. bedroom
3. a. garage
   b. yard
4. a. bathroom
   b. bedroom
5. a. kitchen
   b. living room
6. a. bedroom
   b. basement

15

PRONUNCIATION Reduced *and*

Mr. and Mrs.

Listen. Then say it.	Say it. Then listen.
Mr. and Mrs. Jones	Mr. and Mrs. Lee
Mr. and Mrs. Park	Mr. and Mrs. Miller
Jim and Pam	Walter and Mary
You and Ben	Jim and I

 Draw a picture of your apartment or house. Label the rooms.

 Work with another student. Draw a picture of your classroom. Label all the objects.

CHAPTER SUMMARY

GRAMMAR

SUBJECT PRONOUNS
TO BE + LOCATION

	am	I?
Where	is	he? she? it?
	are	we? you? they?

(I am)	I'm	
(He is) (She is) (It is)	He's She's It's	in the kitchen.
(We are) (You are) (They are)	We're You're They're	

KEY VOCABULARY

CLASSROOM OBJECTS

board	globe
book	map
bookshelf	notebook
bulletin board	pen
chair	pencil
clock	ruler
computer	table
desk	wall
dictionary	

PLACES AT HOME

attic
basement
bathroom
bedroom
dining room
garage
kitchen
living room
yard

PLACES AROUND TOWN

bank
hospital
library
movie theater
park
post office
restaurant
supermarket
zoo

GREETING PEOPLE

Hi. How are you?
Fine. And you?
Fine, thanks.

Present Continuous Tense

- **Everyday Activities**

VOCABULARY PREVIEW

1. eating
2. drinking
3. cooking
4. reading
5. studying

6. teaching
7. singing
8. sleeping
9. swimming
10. planting

11. watching TV
12. listening to music
13. playing cards
14. playing baseball
15. playing the piano

What Are You Doing?

What	am is are	I { he she it } { we you they }	doing?

(I am) (He is) (She is) (It is) (We are) (You are) (They are)	I'm He's She's It's We're You're They're	} eating.

What are you doing?

I'm reading.

What are you doing?

We're cooking.

What are Mary and Fred doing?

They're studying English.

What's Tom doing?

He's eating.

What's Martha doing?

She's watching TV.

What's your dog doing?

It's sleeping.

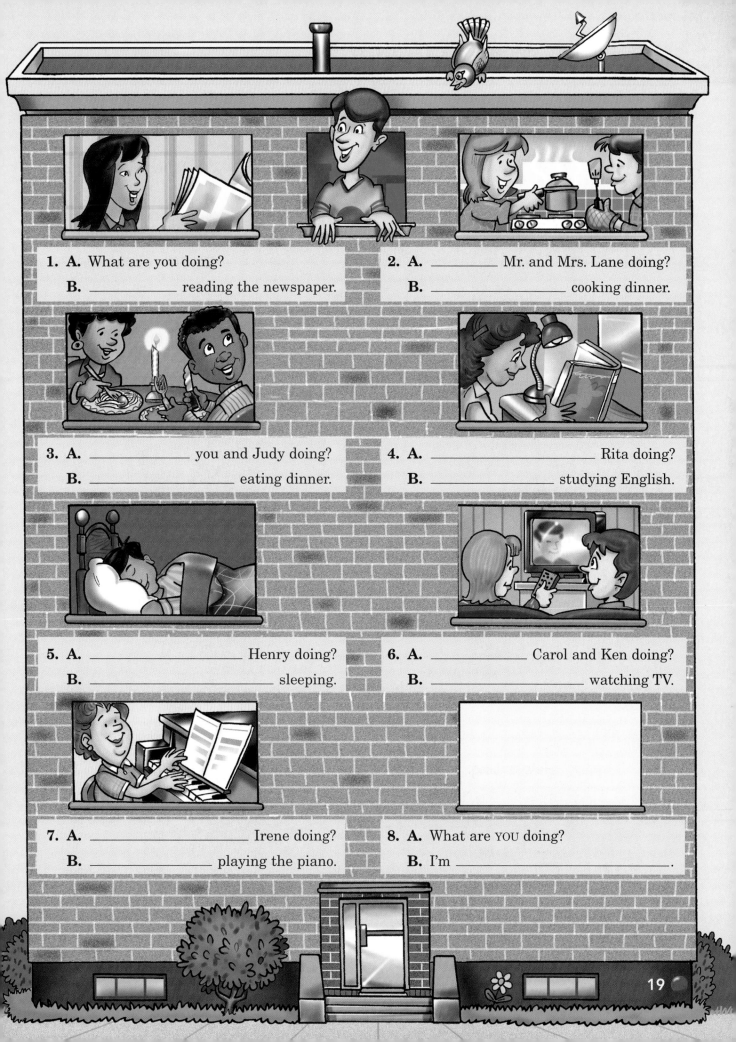

1. **A.** What are you doing?
   B. _____ reading the newspaper.

2. **A.** _____ Mr. and Mrs. Lane doing?
   B. _____ cooking dinner.

3. **A.** _____ you and Judy doing?
   B. _____ eating dinner.

4. **A.** _____ Rita doing?
   B. _____ studying English.

5. **A.** _____ Henry doing?
   B. _____ sleeping.

6. **A.** _____ Carol and Ken doing?
   B. _____ watching TV.

7. **A.** _____ Irene doing?
   B. _____ playing the piano.

8. **A.** What are YOU doing?
   B. I'm _____ .

What's Everybody Doing?

A. Where's Walter?

B. He's in the kitchen.

A. What's he doing?

B. He's eating breakfast.

1. *Karen*
park
eating lunch

2. *Mr. and Mrs. Clark*
dining room
eating dinner

3. *you*
bedroom
playing the guitar

4. *you*
living room
playing cards

5. *Gary and Jane*
yard
playing baseball

6. *Miss Baker*
cafeteria
drinking milk

7. *you*
library
studying English

8. *Ms. Johnson*
classroom
teaching mathematics

9. *Marvin*
bathroom
singing

10. *Martha*
hospital
watching TV

11. *your friend*
park
listening to music

12.

How to Say It!

Checking Understanding

A. Where's *Walter*?
B. He's in the *kitchen*.
A. In the *kitchen*?
B. Yes.

Practice conversations with other students.

IN THE PARK

The Jones family is in the park today. The sun is shining, and the birds are singing. It's a beautiful day!

Mr. Jones is reading the newspaper. Mrs. Jones is listening to the radio. Sally and Patty Jones are studying. And Tommy Jones is playing the guitar.

The Jones family is very happy today. It's a beautiful day, and they're in the park.

AT HOME IN THE YARD

The Chen family is at home in the yard today. The sun is shining, and the birds are singing. It's a beautiful day!

Mr. Chen is planting flowers. Mrs. Chen is drinking lemonade and reading a book. Emily and Jason Chen are playing with the dog. And Jennifer Chen is sleeping.

The Chen family is very happy today. It's a beautiful day, and they're at home in the yard.

✔ READING CHECK-UP

TRUE OR FALSE?

_____ 1. The Jones family is at home in the yard today.

_____ 2. Mrs. Chen is planting flowers.

_____ 3. Patty Jones is studying.

_____ 4. Jason Chen is reading a book.

_____ 5. The Chen family is singing.

_____ 6. The Jones family and the Chen family are very happy today.

Q & A

Using this model, make questions and answers based on the stories on page 22.

A. *What's Mr. Jones doing?*
B. *He's reading the newspaper.*

LISTENING

Listen and choose the correct answer.

1. a. She's studying.
    b. I'm studying.

2. a. He's eating.
    b. She's eating.

3. a. He's watching TV.
    b. She's watching TV.

4. a. We're cooking dinner.
    b. They're cooking dinner.

5. a. We're planting flowers.
    b. They're planting flowers.

6. a. You're playing baseball.
    b. We're playing baseball.

IN YOUR OWN WORDS

FOR WRITING AND DISCUSSION

Mr. and Mrs. Martinez
Alex Martinez
Tina Martinez
Jimmy Martinez

AT THE BEACH

The Martinez family is at the beach today. Using this picture, tell a story about the Martinez family.

23

PRONUNCIATION Reduced *What are & Where are*

Listen. Then say it.

What are you doing?

What are Jim and Jane doing?

Where are Mary and Fred?

Where are you and Judy?

Say it. Then listen.

What are they doing?

What are Carol and Ken doing?

Where are Mr. and Mrs. Lane?

Where are you and Henry?

SIDE by SIDE JOURNAL

What are you doing now?
What are your friends doing?
Write about it in your
journal.

CHAPTER SUMMARY

GRAMMAR

PRESENT CONTINUOUS TENSE

What	am	I	doing?
	is	he she it	
	are	we you they	

(I am)	I'm	eating.
(He is) (She is) (It is)	He's She's It's	
(We are) (You are) (They are)	We're You're They're	

KEY VOCABULARY

EVERYDAY ACTIVITIES

cooking dinner
drinking milk / lemonade
eating breakfast / lunch / dinner
listening to music / the radio
planting flowers
playing cards
playing baseball
playing the guitar / the piano

reading a book / the newspaper
singing
sleeping
studying English
swimming
teaching
watching TV

CHECKING UNDERSTANDING

In the kitchen?

FACT FILE

Titles

Mr. is a title for a man.
Ms., Mrs., and Miss are titles for a woman.

Nicknames

> My name is David.
> My nickname is Dave.

COMMON NICKNAMES

Name	Nickname	Name	Nickname
James	Jim	Elizabeth	Liz, Betty
Peter	Pete	Jennifer	Jenny
Robert	Bob	Judith	Judy
Timothy	Tim	Katherine	Kathy, Kate
Thomas	Tom	Patricia	Patty
William	Bill	Susan	Sue

Global Exchange

SungHee: Hello. My name is Sung Hee. I'm Korean. I'm from Seoul. I'm a student. Right now I'm in my English class. I'm looking for a keypal in a different country.

DanielR: Hi, Sung Hee! My name is Daniel. My nickname is Danny. My last name is Rivera. I'm Mexican. I'm from Mexico City. I'm a student. Right now I'm at home. I'm at my computer, and I'm listening to music. I'm also looking for a keypal. Tell me about your school and your English class.

Send a message over the Internet. Tell about yourself.
Look for a keypal.

I'm playing _____ .

Instruments

 the violin

 the clarinet

 the trumpet

Sports

 soccer

 tennis

 basketball

Games

 chess

 checkers

 tic tac toe

AROUND THE WORLD

Greetings

Right now, all around the world, people are greeting each other in different ways.

They're shaking hands.

They're kissing.

They're bowing.

They're hugging.

How are people in your country greeting each other today?

LISTENING

You have seven messages!

You Have Seven Messages!

Messages

_c_	①	**a.** Mrs. Lane 731–0248
___	②	**b.** Linda Lee 969–0159
___	③	**c.** Henry Drake 427–9168
___	④	**d.** Dad
___	⑤	**e.** Patty
___	⑥	**f.** Jim 682–4630
___	⑦	**g.** Kevin Carter 298–4577

What Are They Saying?

To Be: Short Answers
Possessive Adjectives

- **Everyday Activities**

VOCABULARY PREVIEW

1. brushing
2. cleaning
3. feeding
4. fixing
5. painting
6. reading
7. washing

I'm Fixing My Sink

I	my
he	his
she	her
it	its
we	our
you	your
they	their

Hi! What are you doing?

I'm fixing **my** sink.

What's Bob doing?

He's fixing **his** car.

What's Mary doing?

She's cleaning **her** room.

What are you doing?

We're cleaning **our** apartment.

What are **your** children doing?

They're doing **their** homework.

Are You Busy?

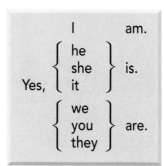

Yes,	I am.
	he / she / it is.
	we / you / they are.

Are you busy?

Yes, I am.
I'm washing my hair.

1. Is Frank busy?
cleaning his apartment

2. Is Helen busy?
feeding her cat

3. Are you busy?
fixing our TV

4. Are Jim and Lisa busy?
painting their bedroom

5. Are you busy?
doing my homework

6. Is Richard busy?
washing his clothes

7. Are Ed and Ruth busy?
painting their garage

8. Is Timmy busy?
feeding his dog

9. Are you busy?
doing our exercises

10. Are you busy?
fixing my bicycle

11. Is Karen busy?
washing her car

12. Is Anwar busy?
cleaning his yard

13. Are your children busy?
brushing their teeth

14. Are you busy?
washing our windows

15. Is Wendy busy?
reading her e-mail

How to Say It!

Attracting Someone's Attention

A. Jane?
B. Yes?
A. What are you doing?
B. I'm *doing* my *exercises*.

Practice conversations with other students.

TALK ABOUT IT! *Where Are They, and What Are They Doing?*

Use these models to talk about the picture with other students in your class.

A. Where's *Mr. Molina*?	**A.** Where are *Mr. and Mrs. Sharp*?
B. *He's* in the *park*.	**B.** They're in the *laundromat*.
A. What's *he* doing?	**A.** What are they doing?
B. *He's listening to the radio.*	**B.** They're *washing their clothes*.

READING

A BUSY DAY

Everybody at 159 River Street is very busy today. Mr. Price is cleaning his bedroom. Ms. Hunter is painting her bathroom. Ricky Gomez is feeding his cat. Mr. and Mrs. Wong are washing their clothes. Mrs. Martin is doing her exercises. And Judy and Larry Clark are fixing their car.

I'm busy, too. I'm washing my windows . . . and of course, I'm watching all my neighbors. It's a very busy day at 159 River Street.

✔ READING *CHECK-UP*

TRUE OR FALSE?

_____ **1.** Mr. Price is in his bedroom.

_____ **2.** Ricky is eating.

_____ **3.** Mr. and Mrs. Clark are in their apartment.

_____ **4.** Mrs. Martin is doing her exercises.

_____ **5.** Their address is 195 River Street.

Q & A

Using this model, make questions and answers based on the story.

A. *What's Mr. Price doing?*
B. *He's cleaning his bedroom.*

LISTENING

Listen and choose the correct answer.

1. a. The newspaper.
   b. Breakfast.

2. a. Her e-mail.
   b. Dinner.

3. a. The dining room.
   b. Soccer.

4. a. Their kitchen.
   b. Basketball.

5. a. TV.
   b. My clothes.

6. a. His neighbors.
   b. His windows.

IN YOUR OWN WORDS

FOR WRITING AND DISCUSSION

A BUSY DAY

Everybody at 320 Main Street is very busy today. Tell a story about them, using this picture and the story on page 32 as a guide.

PRONUNCIATION Deleted *h*

Listen. Then say it.

She's fixing her car.

She's cleaning her room.

He's feeding his dog.

He's washing his windows.

Say it. Then listen.

He's painting his apartment.

She's doing her homework.

He's brushing his teeth.

She's reading her e-mail.

Go to a place in your community—a park, a library, a supermarket, or someplace else. Look at the people. What are they doing? Write about it in your journal.

CHAPTER SUMMARY

GRAMMAR

TO BE: SHORT ANSWERS

	I	am.
Yes,	he she it	is.
	we you they	are.

POSSESSIVE ADJECTIVES

I'm		my	
He's		his	
She's		her	
It's	cleaning	its	room.
We're		our	
You're		your	
They're		their	

KEY VOCABULARY

EVERYDAY ACTIVITIES

brushing *my* teeth
cleaning *his* apartment / garage / living room / room / yard
doing *her* exercises / homework
feeding *our* cat / dog
fixing *your* bicycle / car / sink / TV
painting *their* bathroom / bedroom / kitchen / living room
washing *my* car / clothes / hair / windows

GREETING PEOPLE

Hi!

ATTRACTING ATTENTION

Jane?

To Be: Yes/No Questions
Short Answers
Adjectives
Possessive Nouns

- **Describing People and Things**
- **Weather**

VOCABULARY PREVIEW

1. tall – short
2. young – old
3. heavy / fat – thin
4. new – old

5. married – single
6. handsome – ugly
7. beautiful / pretty – ugly
8. large / big – small / little

9. noisy / loud – quiet
10. expensive – cheap
11. easy – difficult
12. rich – poor

Tall or Short?

(I am)	I'm	
(He is)	He's	
(She is)	She's	
(It is)	It's	tall.
(We are)	We're	
(You are)	You're	
(They are)	They're	

A. Is Bob tall or short?

B. He's tall.

A. Is Bill tall or short?

B. He's short.

Bob   Bill

Ask and answer these questions.

Kate   Peggy

1. Is Kate young or old?
2. Is Peggy young or old?

Howard   Mike

3. Is Howard heavy or thin?
4. Is Mike fat or thin?

Howard's car   Mike's car

5. Is Howard's car new or old?
6. Is Mike's car new or old?

Gloria   Jennifer

7. Is Gloria married or single?
8. Is Jennifer married or single?

9. Is Robert handsome or ugly?

10. Is Captain Crook handsome or ugly?

11. Is Vanessa beautiful or ugly?

12. Is Hilda pretty or ugly?

Robert's house George's apartment

Kate's neighbors Peggy's neighbors

13. Is Robert's house large or small?

14. Is George's apartment big or little?

15. Are Kate's neighbors noisy or quiet?

16. Are Peggy's neighbors loud or quiet?

the food at the the food at
Plaza Restaurant Burger Town

the questions in the questions in
Chapter 5 Chapter 17

17. Is the food at the Plaza Restaurant expensive or cheap?

18. Is the food at Burger Town expensive or cheap?

19. Are the questions in Chapter 5 easy or difficult?

20. Are the questions in Chapter 17 easy or difficult?

Marvin Larry

21. Is Marvin rich or poor?

22. Is Larry rich or poor?

Now ask and answer your own questions.

37

Tell Me About . . .

Am	I		
Is	he she it	tall?	
Are	we you they		

Yes,	I	am.
	he she it	is.
	we you they	are.

No,	I'm	not.
	he she it	isn't.
	we you they	aren't.

Are you married?

No, I'm not. I'm single.

Tell me about your new car. Is it large?

No, it isn't. It's small.

Tell me about your new neighbors. Are they quiet?

No, they aren't. They're noisy.

1. **A.** Tell me about your computer.
   _____ new?
   B. No, _____. _____.

2. **A.** Tell me about your new boss.
   _____ young?
   B. No, _____. _____.

3. A. Tell me about your neighbors.

_____ noisy?

B. No, _____. _____.

4. A. Tell me about the Plaza Restaurant.

_____ cheap?

B. No, _____. _____.

5. A. Tell me about your brother.

_____ tall?

B. No, _____. _____.

6. A. Tell me about your sister.

_____ single?

B. No, _____. _____.

7. A. Tell me about Nancy's cat.

_____ pretty?

B. No, _____. _____.

8. A. Tell me about Ron and Betty's dog.

_____ little?

B. No, _____. _____.

9. A. Tell me about the questions in your English book.

_____ difficult?

B. No, _____. _____.

10. A. Tell me about Santa Claus.

_____ thin?

B. No, _____. _____.

How's the Weather Today?

How's the weather today in YOUR city?

How to Say It!

Calling Someone You Know on the Telephone

A. Hello.

B. Hello. Is this *Julie*?

A. Yes, it is.

B. Hi, *Julie*. This is *Anna*.

A. Hi, *Anna*. . . .

Practice conversations with other students.

The Weather Is Terrible Here!

A. Hi, Jack. This is Jim. I'm calling from Miami.

B. From Miami? What are you doing in Miami?

A. I'm on vacation.

B. How's the weather in Miami? Is it sunny?

A. No, it isn't. It's raining.

B. Is it hot?

A. No, it isn't. It's cold.

B. Are you having a good time?

A. No, I'm not. I'm having a TERRIBLE time. The weather is TERRIBLE here!

B. I'm sorry to hear that.

A. Hi, _____. This is _____. I'm calling from _____.

B. From _____? What are you doing in _____?

A. I'm on vacation.

B. How's the weather in _____? Is it _____?

A. No, it isn't. It's _____.

B. Is it _____?

A. No, it isn't. It's _____.

B. Are you having a good time?

A. No, I'm not. I'm having a TERRIBLE time. The weather is TERRIBLE here!

B. I'm sorry to hear that.

1. *British Columbia*
cool?
snowing?

2. *Tahiti*
hot?
sunny?

You're on vacation, and the weather is terrible! Call a student in your class. Use the conversation above as a guide.

DEAR MOTHER

Royal Sludge Hotel

Dear Mother,

I'm writing from our hotel at Sludge Beach. Ralph and I are on vacation with the children for a few days. We're happy to be here, but to tell the truth, we're having a few problems.

The weather isn't very good. In fact, it's cold and cloudy. Right now I'm looking out the window, and it's raining cats and dogs.

The children aren't very happy. In fact, they're bored and they're having a terrible time. Right now they're sitting on the bed, playing tic tac toe and watching TV.

The restaurants here are expensive, and the food isn't very good. In fact, Ralph is at a clinic right now. He's having problems with his stomach.

All the other hotels here are beautiful and new. Our hotel is ugly, and it's very, very old. In fact, right now a repairperson is fixing the bathroom sink.

So, Mother, we're having a few problems here at Sludge Beach, but we're happy. We're happy to be on vacation, and we're happy to be together.

See you soon.

Love,

Ethel

✔ READING *CHECK-UP*

True or False?

_____ 1. The weather is beautiful.

_____ 2. The children are happy.

_____ 3. The children are watching TV.

_____ 4. The restaurants are cheap.

_____ 5. Ralph is at the hotel right now.

_____ 6. Their hotel is old.

_____ 7. A repairperson is fixing the window.

_____ 8. Ethel is watching the cats and dogs.

LISTENING

What's the Answer?

Listen and choose the correct answer.

1. a. It's large.   b. It's heavy.
2. a. It's married.   b. It's beautiful.
3. a. They're quiet.   b. They're sunny.
4. a. It's young.   b. It's warm.
5. a. It's small.   b. It's easy.
6. a. It's good.   b. It's raining.

True or False?

Listen to the conversation. Then answer *True* or *False*.

1. Louise is calling Betty.
2. The weather is hot and sunny.
3. The hotel is old.
4. The food is very good.
5. Louise is watching TV.

43

PRONUNCIATION   Yes/No Questions with *or*

Listen. Then say it.

Is Bob tall or short?

Is Kate young or old?

Are they noisy or quiet?

Is it hot or cold?

Say it. Then listen.

Is the car new or old?

Are you married or single?

Is it sunny or cloudy?

Are they large or small?

SIDE by SIDE JOURNAL

How's the weather today?
What are you doing now?
Write a letter to a friend
and tell about it.

May 20, 20__
Dear Mm m.
Sincerely,

CHAPTER SUMMARY

GRAMMAR

TO BE: YES / NO QUESTIONS

Am	I	
Is	he she it	tall?
Are	we you they	

TO BE: SHORT ANSWERS

	I	am.
Yes,	he she it	is.
	we you they	are.

	I'm	not.
No,	he she it	isn't.
	we you they	aren't.

POSSESSIVE NOUNS

Robert**'s** house

Peggy**'s** neighbors

George**'s** apartment

KEY VOCABULARY

DESCRIBING PEOPLE AND THINGS

tall	short	large	small
young	old	big	little
new	old	noisy/loud	quiet
heavy/fat	thin	expensive	cheap
married	single	easy	difficult
handsome	ugly	rich	poor
beautiful/pretty	ugly		

WEATHER

It's sunny.	It's hot.
It's cloudy.	It's warm.
It's raining.	It's cool.
It's snowing.	It's cold.

To Be: Review
Present Continuous Tense: Review
Prepositions of Location

- **Family Members**
- **Describing Activities and Events**

VOCABULARY PREVIEW

1. wife	**children**	**grandparents**	**grandchildren**	13. aunt
2. husband	5. daughter	9. grandmother	11. granddaughter	14. uncle
	6. son	10. grandfather	12. grandson	15. niece
parents	7. sister			16. nephew
3. mother	8. brother			17. cousin
4. father				

My Favorite Photographs

A. Who is he?

B. He's my father.

A. What's his name?

B. His name is Paul.

A. Where is he?

B. He's in Paris.

A. What's he doing?

B. He's standing in front of the Eiffel Tower.

Using these questions, talk about the following photographs.

Who is he?
What's his name?
Where is he?
What's he doing?

Who is she?
What's her name?
Where is she?
What's she doing?

Who are they?
What are their names?
Where are they?
What are they doing?

1. *my mother*
   in the park
   riding her bicycle

2. *my parents*
   in the dining room
   having dinner

3. *my son*
at the beach
swimming

4. *my daughter*
in front of our house
washing her car

5. *my wife*
in the yard
planting flowers

6. *my husband*
in our living room
sleeping on the sofa

7. *my sister and brother*
in the kitchen
baking a cake

8. *my grandmother and grandfather*
at my wedding
crying

9. *my aunt and uncle*
in Washington, D.C.
standing in front of the White House

10. *my cousin*
in front of his apartment building
skateboarding

11. *my niece*
at school
acting in a play

12. *my nephew*
in his bedroom
sitting on his bed and playing the guitar

13. *my friend*
in his apartment
playing a game on his computer

14. *my friends*
at my birthday party
singing and dancing

ON YOUR OWN *Your Favorite Photographs*

This is a photograph of my sister and me. My sister's name is Amanda. We're in the park. Amanda is feeding the birds, and I'm sitting on a bench and listening to music.

Bring in your favorite photographs to class. Talk about them with other students. Ask the other students about *their* favorite photographs.

ARTHUR IS VERY ANGRY

It's late at night. Arthur is sitting on his bed, and he's looking at his clock. His neighbors are making a lot of noise, and Arthur is VERY angry.

The people in Apartment 2 are dancing. The man in Apartment 3 is vacuuming his rug. The woman in Apartment 4 is playing the drums. The teenagers in Apartment 5 are listening to loud music. The dog in Apartment 6 is barking. And the people in Apartment 7 are having a big argument.

It's very late, and Arthur is tired and angry. What a terrible night!

✔ READING *CHECK-UP*

Q & A

Using this model, make questions and answers based on the story.

   A. *What's the man in Apartment 3 doing?*
   B. *He's vacuuming his rugs.*

CHOOSE

1. Arthur's neighbors are _____.
   a. noisy
   b. angry

2. The man in Apartment 3 is _____.
   a. painting
   b. cleaning

3. The people in Apartment 5 are _____.
   a. young
   b. old

4. The dog in Apartment 6 isn't _____.
   a. sleeping
   b. making noise

5. The woman in Apartment 4 is _____.
   a. playing cards
   b. playing music

6. Arthur isn't very _____.
   a. happy
   b. tired

TOM'S WEDDING DAY

Today is a very special day. It's my wedding day, and all my family and friends are here. Everybody is having a wonderful time.

My wife, Jane, is standing in front of the fireplace. She's wearing a beautiful white wedding gown. Uncle Harry is taking her photograph, and Aunt Emma is crying. (She's very sentimental.)

The band is playing my favorite popular music. My mother is dancing with Jane's father, and Jane's mother is dancing with my father.

My sister and Jane's brother are standing in the yard and eating wedding cake. Our grandparents are sitting in the corner and talking about "the good old days."

Everybody is having a good time. People are singing, dancing, and laughing, and our families are getting to know each other. It's a very special day.

✔ READING *CHECK-UP*

WHAT'S THE ANSWER?

1. Where is Jane standing?
2. What's she wearing?
3. What's Uncle Harry doing?

4. What's Aunt Emma doing?
5. What's Tom's mother doing?
6. What are their grandparents doing?

LISTENING

QUIET OR NOISY?

Listen to the sentence. Are the people quiet or noisy?

1. a. quiet   b. noisy
2. a. quiet   b. noisy
3. a. quiet   b. noisy
4. a. quiet   b. noisy
5. a. quiet   b. noisy
6. a. quiet   b. noisy

WHAT DO YOU HEAR?

Listen to the sound. What do you hear? Choose the correct answer.

1. a. They're studying.   b. They're singing.
2. a. He's crying.   b. He's doing his exercises.
3. a. She's vacuuming.   b. She's washing her clothes.
4. a. They're barking.   b. They're laughing.
5. a. She's playing the piano.   b. She's playing the drums.

IN YOUR OWN WORDS

FOR WRITING AND DISCUSSION

JESSICA'S BIRTHDAY PARTY

Today is a very special day. It's Jessica's birthday party, and all her family and friends are there. Using this picture, tell a story about her party.

How to Say It!

Introducing People

A. I'd like to introduce *my brother*.
B. Nice to meet you.
C. Nice to meet you, too.

Practice conversations with other students.

PRONUNCIATION *Stressed and Unstressed Words*

Listen. Then say it.

He's playing the guitar.

She's acting in a play.

She's riding her bicycle.

He's sleeping on the sofa.

Say it. Then listen.

We're baking a cake.

They're sitting in the yard.

He's washing his car.

She's sitting on her bed.

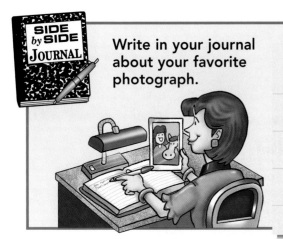

SIDE by SIDE JOURNAL

Write in your journal about your favorite photograph.

This is a photograph of _____.

In this photograph, _____.

It's my favorite photograph because _____.

CHAPTER SUMMARY

GRAMMAR

TO BE

Who is	he? she?
Who are	they?

He's my father. She's my wife.
They're my parents.

PRESENT CONTINUOUS TENSE

What's	he she	doing?
What are	they	doing?

He's She's	sleeping.
They're	swimming.

PREPOSITIONS OF LOCATION

She's **in** the park.	He's sitting **on** his bed.
He's **at** the beach.	We're **in front of** our house.

KEY VOCABULARY

FAMILY MEMBERS

mother	grandmother	wife
father	grandfather	husband
parents	grandparents	aunt
son	grandson	uncle
daughter	granddaughter	niece
children	grandchildren	nephew
brother	sister	cousin

EVERYDAY ACTIVITIES

acting	laughing
baking	riding
crying	skateboarding
dancing	talking
having *dinner*	vacuuming

INTRODUCING SOMEONE

I'd like to introduce _____.
Nice to meet you.
Nice to meet you, too.

SIDE *by* SIDE **Gazette**

A Family Tree

Betty and Henry Wilson's family tree is very large

Betty and Henry

Sally   Jack   Linda   Patty   Tom

Jimmy   Sarah   Julie   Kevin

A family tree is a diagram of the people in a family. This is the Wilson family tree. All the members of the Wilson family are on this family tree—parents, children, grandparents, grandchildren, aunts, uncles, cousins, nieces, and nephews.

Betty and Henry are the parents of Sally, Linda, and Tom. Linda is single. Sally is married. Her husband's name is Jack. Sally and Jack are the parents of Jimmy and Sarah. Jimmy is their son, and Sarah is their daughter.

Tom is also married. His wife's name is Patty. Patty and Tom are the parents of Julie and Kevin. Julie is their daughter, and Kevin is their son.

Jimmy, Sarah, Julie, and Kevin are cousins. They are also the grandchildren of Betty and Henry. (Betty and Henry are their grandparents.)

Jack is Julie and Kevin's uncle. Sally is their aunt. Tom is Jimmy and Sarah's uncle. Patty is their aunt. Linda is also the aunt of Jimmy, Sarah, Julie, and Kevin.

Jimmy is the nephew of Linda, Patty, and Tom. Sarah is their niece. Julie is the niece of Sally, Jack, and Linda. Kevin is their nephew.

Draw your family tree. Then write about it.

BUILD YOUR VOCABULARY!

Classroom Activities

I'm _____ .

 ■ reading

 ■ writing

 ■ raising my hand

 ■ opening my book

 ■ closing my book

 ■ erasing the board

 ■ using a calculator

Today's Weather

_d_ ❶ hot   a. Atlanta

___ ❷ snowing   b. Chicago

___ ❸ warm and sunny   c. Toronto

___ ❹ cool and sunny   d. Honolulu

___ ❺ cold and cloudy   e. Los Angeles

AROUND THE WORLD

Extended and Nuclear Families

This is an **extended family**. The grandparents, parents, and children are all together in one apartment. An uncle, an aunt, and two cousins are in another apartment in the same building. Extended families are very common around the world.

This is a **nuclear family**. Only the mother, father, and children are in this home. The grandparents, aunts, uncles, and cousins are in different homes. Nuclear families are very common in many countries.

Is your family a nuclear family or an extended family? Which type of family is common in your country? In your opinion, what are some good things and bad things about these different types of families?

Global Exchange

Ken425: It's a beautiful day in our city today. It's warm and sunny. The people in my family are very busy. My brother and sister are cleaning our apartment. My mother is washing the windows, and my father is fixing the bathroom sink. I'm cooking dinner for my family. How about you? What's the weather today? What are you doing? What are other people in your family doing?

Send a message to a keypal. Tell about the weather, and tell about what you and others are doing today.

FACT FILE

Family Relationships

wife's mother husband's mother }	=	mother-in-law
wife's father husband's father }	=	father-in-law
son's wife	=	daughter-in-law
daughter's husband	=	son-in-law
wife's sister husband's sister }	=	sister-in-law
wife's brother husband's brother }	=	brother-in-law

What Are They Saying?

Prepositions
There Is/There Are
Singular/Plural: Introduction

- **Places Around Town**
- **Locating Places**
- **Describing Neighborhoods**
- **Describing Apartments**

VOCABULARY PREVIEW

1. bakery	6. clinic	11. hotel
2. barber shop	7. department store	12. laundromat
3. book store	8. drug store	13. school
4. bus station	9. hair salon	14. train station
5. cafeteria	10. health club	15. video store

Where's the Restaurant?

A. Where's the restaurant?
B. It's **next to** the bank.

A. Where's the school?
B. It's **between** the library and the park.

A. Where's the supermarket?
B. It's **across from** the movie theater.

A. Where's the post office?
B. It's **around the corner from** the hospital.

1. Where's the bank?

3. Where's the restaurant?

5. Where's the hotel?

7. Where's the clinic?

2. Where's the post office?

4. Where's the hospital?

6. Where's the gas station?

8. Where's the bakery?

Is There a Laundromat in This Neighborhood?

> **There's (There is)** a bank on Main Street.
> **Is there** a bank on Main Street?

A. Excuse me. Is there a laundromat in this neighborhood?

B. Yes. There's a laundromat on Main Street, next to the supermarket.

1. *drug store?*

2. *clinic?*

3. *department store?*

4. *hair salon?*

5. *book store?*

6. *post office?*

How to Say It!

Expressing Gratitude

A. Thank you. / Thanks.

B. You're welcome.

Practice some conversations on this page again.
Express gratitude at the end of each conversation.

| Is there . . . ? | Yes, there is.
No, there isn't. |

Is there a restaurant in your neighborhood?

No, there isn't.

Is there a cafeteria in your neighborhood?

Yes, there is.

Where is it?

It's on Central Avenue, across from the bank.

Draw a simple map of your neighborhood. With another student, ask and answer questions about your neighborhoods.

Some places you can talk about:

bakery	clinic	hospital	post office
bank	department store	hotel	restaurant
barber shop	drug store	laundromat	school
book store	fire station	library	supermarket
bus station	gas station	movie theater	train station
cafeteria	hair salon	park	video store
church	health club	police station	

Is There a Stove in the Kitchen?

A. Is there a stove in the kitchen?

B. Yes, there is. There's a very nice stove in the kitchen.

A. Oh, good.

A. Is there a refrigerator in the kitchen?

B. No, there isn't.

A. Oh, I see.

1. *a window in the kitchen?*
Yes, . . .

2. *a fire escape?*
No, . . .

3. *a closet in the bedroom?*
Yes, . . .

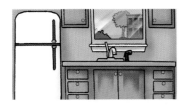

4. *an elevator* in the building?*
No, . . .

5. *an air conditioner* in the bedroom?*
Yes, . . .

6. *a superintendent in the building?*
No, . . .

7. *a bus stop near the building?*
No, . . .

8. *a jacuzzi in the bathroom?*
Yes, . . .

* **a** stove   **an** elevator
   a closet   **an** air conditioner

How Many Bedrooms Are There in the Apartment?

| How many windows **are there** in the bedroom? | **There's** one window in the bedroom.
There are two windows in the bedroom. |

A. Tell me, how many bedrooms are there in the apartment?

B. There are two bedrooms in the apartment.

A. Two bedrooms?

B. Yes. That's right.

1. *floors*
building

2. *windows*
living room

3. *closets*
apartment

4. *apartments*
building

5. *washing machines*
basement

6. *bathrooms*
apartment

* two and a half

An Apartment Building

SUPERINTENDENT

BUS STOP

ROLE PLAY   *Looking for an Apartment*

Is there a window?	Are there any windows?
Yes, there is. / No, there isn't.	Yes, there are. / No, there aren't.

You're looking for a new apartment. Practice with another student. Ask questions about the apartment on page 61.

Ask the landlord:

1. a stove in the kitchen?
2. a refrigerator in the kitchen?
3. a superintendent in the building?
4. an elevator in the building?
5. a fire escape?
6. a satellite dish on the roof?
7. a mailbox near the building?
8. a bus stop near the building?

Ask a tenant in the building:

9. children in the building?
10. cats in the building?
11. mice in the basement?
12. cockroaches in the building?
13. broken windows in the building?
14. holes in the walls?
15. washing machines in the basement?

Ask the landlord:

16. rooms—in the apartment?
17. floors—in the building?
18. closets—in the bedroom?
19. windows—in the living room?

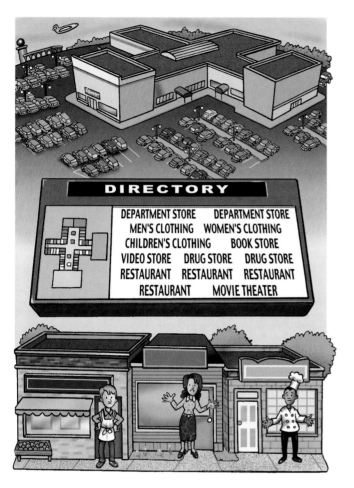

THE NEW SHOPPING MALL

Everybody in Brewster is talking about the city's new shopping mall. The mall is outside the city, next to the Brewster airport. There are more than one hundred stores in the mall.

There are two big department stores. There are many clothing stores for men, women, and children. There's a book store, and there's a video store. There are two drug stores, and there are four restaurants. There's even a large movie theater.

Almost all the people in Brewster are happy that their city's new shopping mall is now open. But some people aren't happy. The owners of the small stores in the old center of town are very upset. They're upset because many people aren't shopping in the stores in the center of town. They're shopping at the new mall.

✔ READING *CHECK-UP*

CHOOSE

1. Everybody in Brewster is _____.
   a. at the airport
   b. outside the city
   c. talking about the mall

2. In the mall, there are _____.
   a. two video stores
   b. two drug stores
   c. two restaurants

3. In the mall, there are _____.
   a. book stores and cafeterias
   b. restaurants and drug stores
   c. clothing stores and video stores

4. The store owners in the center of town are upset because _____.
   a. people aren't shopping in their stores
   b. people aren't shopping at the mall
   c. they're very old

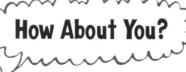

How About You?

Is there a shopping mall in your city or town?
Are there small stores in your city or town?
Tell about stores where you live.

AMY'S APARTMENT BUILDING

Amy's apartment building is in the center of town. Amy is very happy there because the building is in a very convenient place.

Across from the building, there's a bank, a post office, and a restaurant. Next to the building, there's a drug store and a laundromat. Around the corner from the building, there are two supermarkets.

There's a lot of noise near Amy's apartment building. There are a lot of cars on the street, and there are a lot of people on the sidewalks all day and all night.

However, Amy isn't very upset about the noise in her neighborhood. Her building is in the center of town. It's a very busy place, but it's a convenient place to live.

✓ READING *CHECK-UP*

WHAT'S THE ANSWER?

1. Where is Amy's apartment building?
2. What's across from her building?
3. Is there a laundromat near her building?
4. Why is there a lot of noise near Amy's building?
5. Why is Amy happy there?

TRUE OR FALSE?

1. Amy's apartment is in a convenient place.
2. There's a drug store around the corner from her building.
3. There are two supermarkets in her neighborhood.
4. There are a lot of cars on the sidewalk.
5. The center of town is very noisy.

How About You?

Tell about YOUR neighborhood.
Is it convenient? Is it very busy?
Is it noisy or quiet?

IN YOUR OWN WORDS

FOR WRITING AND DISCUSSION

EDWARD'S APARTMENT BUILDING

Edward's apartment building is in the center of town. Edward is very happy there because the building is in a very convenient place. Using this picture, tell about Edward's neighborhood.

LISTENING

WHAT PLACES DO YOU HEAR?

Listen and choose the correct places.

Example:	(a.) supermarket	b. school	(c.) video store
1.	a. park	b. bank	c. laundromat
2.	a. fire station	b. police station	c. gas station
3.	a. school	b. department store	c. clothing store
4.	a. bank	b. drug store	c. book store
5.	a. hotel	b. hair salon	c. hospital

TRUE OR FALSE?

Listen to the conversation. Then answer *True* or *False*.

1. There are four rooms in the apartment.
2. There are two closets in the bedroom.
3. There are four windows in the kitchen.
4. There's a superintendent in the building.
5. There are three washing machines.
6. There's an elevator in the building.

PRONUNCIATION *Rising Intonation to Check Understanding*

Listen. Then say it.	Say it. Then listen.
Two bedrooms?	Three windows?
Five closets?	Twenty floors?
Next to the bank?	Across from the clinic?
On Main Street?	On Central Avenue?

SIDE *by* SIDE JOURNAL

In your journal, write about your apartment building or home. Tell about the building and the neighborhood.

CHAPTER SUMMARY

GRAMMAR

THERE IS/THERE ARE

There's one window in the bedroom.

Is there a laundromat in this neighborhood?
  Yes, there is.
  No, there isn't.

There are two windows in the bedroom.

Are there any children in the building?
  Yes, there are.
  No, there aren't.

PREPOSITIONS

It's next to the bank.
It's across from the movie theater.
It's between the library and the park.
It's around the corner from the hospital.

SINGULAR/PLURAL: INTRODUCTION

There's one bedroom in the apartment.
There are two bedrooms in the apartment.

KEY VOCABULARY

PLACES AROUND TOWN

airport	drug store	police station
bakery	fire station	post office
bank	gas station	restaurant
barber shop	hair salon	school
book store	health club	shopping mall
bus station	hospital	supermarket
cafeteria	hotel	train station
church	laundromat	video store
clinic	library	zoo
clothing store	movie theater	
department store	park	

HOUSING

air conditioner	floor
apartment building	jacuzzi
building	mailbox
bus stop	refrigerator
closet	stove
elevator	superintendent
fire escape	washing machine

Singular/Plural
Adjectives
This/That/These/Those

- **Clothing**
- **Colors**

- **Shopping for Clothing**

VOCABULARY PREVIEW

1. shirt	6. jacket	11. pants
2. coat	7. suit	12. jeans
3. dress	8. tie	13. pajamas
4. skirt	9. belt	14. shoes
5. blouse	10. sweater	15. socks

Clothing

1. shirt	**8.** earring	**15.** hat	**21.** suit
2. tie	**9.** necklace	**16.** coat	**22.** watch
3. jacket	**10.** blouse	**17.** glove	**23.** umbrella
4. belt	**11.** bracelet	**18.** purse /	**24.** sweater
5. pants	**12.** skirt	pocketbook	**25.** mitten
6. sock	**13.** briefcase	**19.** dress	**26.** jeans
7. shoe	**14.** stocking	**20.** glasses	**27.** boot

Shirts Are Over There

SINGULAR/PLURAL*

a shirt – shirt**s**
a coat – coat**s**
a hat – hat**s**
a belt – belt**s**

a tie – tie**s**
an umbrella – umbrella**s**
a sweater – sweater**s**

a dress – dress**es**
a watch – watch**es**
a blouse – blous**es**
a necklace – necklac**es**

A. Excuse me.
I'm looking for **a shirt**.

B. **Shirts** are over there.

A. Thanks.

A. Excuse me.
I'm looking for **a tie**.

B. **Ties** are over there.

A. Thanks.

A. Excuse me.
I'm looking for **a dress**.

B. **Dresses** are over there.

A. Thanks.

1.

2.

3.

4.

5.

6.

7.

8.

Put these words in the correct column.

| boots | briefcases | earrings | glasses | gloves | pants | purses | shoes | socks |

s	**z**	**iz**
boots		

* Some irregular plurals you know are:

a man – men   a child – children   a tooth – teeth
a woman – women   a person – people   a mouse – mice

I'm Looking for a Jacket

COLORS

red   orange   yellow   green   blue   purple   black   silver

pink   gray   white   gold   brown

A. May I help you?

B. Yes, please. I'm looking for a jacket.

A. Here's a nice jacket.

B. But this is a PURPLE jacket!

A. That's okay. Purple jackets are very POPULAR this year.

A. May I help you?

B. Yes, please. I'm looking for a _____.

A. Here's a nice _____.

B. But this is a _____ _____!

A. That's okay. _____ _____s are very POPULAR this year.

1. *red*

2. *white*

3. *pink*

4. *orange*

5. *yellow*

6. *green and purple*

7. *striped*

8. *polka dot*

I'm Looking for a Pair of Gloves

pair of shoes/socks . . .

A. Can I help you?

B. Yes, please. I'm looking for a pair of gloves.

A. Here's a nice pair of gloves.

B. But these are GREEN gloves!

A. That's okay. Green gloves are very POPULAR this year.

A. Can I help you?

B. Yes, please. I'm looking for a pair of _gloves_.

A. Here's a nice pair of _gloves_.

B. But these are _____ _____s!

A. That's okay. _____ _____s are very POPULAR this year.

1. *yellow*

2. *blue*

3. *pink*

4. *orange*

5. *striped*

6. *green*

7. *red, white, and blue*

8. *polka dot*

How About You?

What are you wearing today?
What are the students in your class wearing today?
What's your favorite color?

NOTHING TO WEAR

Fred is upset this morning. He's looking for something to wear to work, but there's nothing in his closet.

He's looking for a clean shirt, but all his shirts are dirty. He's looking for a sports jacket, but all his sports jackets are at the dry cleaner's. He's looking for a pair of pants, but all the pants in his closet are ripped. And he's looking for a pair of socks, but all his socks are on the clothesline, and it's raining!

Fred is having a difficult time this morning. He's getting dressed for work, but his closet is empty, and there's nothing to wear.

✔ READING *CHECK-UP*

CHOOSE

1. Fred's closet is _____.
   a. upset
   b. empty

2. Fred is _____.
   a. at home
   b. at work

3. Fred's shirts are _____.
   a. dirty
   b. clean

4. He's looking for a pair of _____.
   a. jackets
   b. pants

5. The weather is _____.
   a. not very good
   b. beautiful

6. Fred is upset because _____.
   a. he's getting dressed
   b. there's nothing to wear

WHICH WORD DOESN'T BELONG?

Example:	a. socks	b. stockings	c. jeans	d. shoes
1.	a. sweater	b. jacket	c. briefcase	d. coat
2.	a. necklace	b. belt	c. bracelet	d. earrings
3.	a. blouse	b. skirt	c. dress	d. tie
4.	a. clean	b. green	c. gray	d. blue
5.	a. pants	b. shoes	c. earrings	d. blouse

Excuse Me. I Think That's My Jacket.

This/That is	These/Those are

1. hat

2. boots

3. coat

4. pen

5. pencils

6. umbrella

7. sunglasses

8.

Lost and Found

A. Is this your umbrella?

B. No, it isn't.

A. Are you sure?

B. Yes. THAT umbrella is BROWN, and MY umbrella is BLACK.

A. Are these your boots?

B. No, they aren't.

A. Are you sure?

B. Yes. THOSE boots are DIRTY, and MY boots are CLEAN.

Make up conversations, using colors and other adjectives you know.

1. *watch*
2. *gloves*
3. *briefcase*
4. *mittens*
5. _____

How to Say It!

Complimenting

A. That's a very nice *hat*!
B. Thank you.

A. Those are very nice *boots*!
B. Thank you.

Practice conversations with other students.

READING

HOLIDAY SHOPPING

Mrs. Miller is doing her holiday shopping. She's looking for gifts for her family, but she's having a lot of trouble.

She's looking for a brown umbrella for her son, but all the umbrellas are black. She's looking for a gray raincoat for her daughter, but all the raincoats are yellow. She's looking for a cotton sweater for her husband, but all the sweaters are wool.

She's looking for an inexpensive bracelet for her sister, but all the bracelets are expensive. She's looking for a leather purse for her mother, but all the purses are vinyl. And she's looking for a polka dot tie for her father, but all the ties are striped.

Poor Mrs. Miller is very frustrated. She's looking for special gifts for all the special people in her family, but she's having a lot of trouble.

✔ READING *CHECK-UP*

Q & A

Mrs. Miller is in the department store. Using this model, create dialogs based on the story.

A. Excuse me. I'm looking for *a brown umbrella* for my *son*.
B. I'm sorry. All our *umbrellas* are *black*.

LISTENING

WHAT'S THE WORD?

Listen and choose the correct answer.

1. a. blouse   b. dress
2. a. shoes   b. boots
3. a. necklace   b. bracelet
4. a. coat   b. raincoat
5. a. socks   b. stockings
6. a. shirt   b. skirt

WHICH WORD DO YOU HEAR?

Listen and choose the correct answer.

1. a. jacket   b. jackets
2. a. belt   b. belts
3. a. sweater   b. sweaters
4. a. suit   b. suits
5. a. shoe   b. shoes
6. a. tie   b. ties

Listen. Then say it.

But this is a PURPLE jacket!

Green gloves are very POPULAR this year.

I think this is MY jacket.

THAT umbrella is BROWN, and
MY umbrella is BLACK.

Say it. Then listen.

But these are YELLOW shoes!

Striped socks are very POPULAR this year.

I think these are MY glasses.

THOSE boots are DIRTY, and
MY boots are CLEAN.

SIDE by SIDE JOURNAL

What are you wearing today? Tell about the clothing and the colors. Write about it in your journal.

CHAPTER SUMMARY

GRAMMAR

SINGULAR/PLURAL

[s]	I'm looking for **a coat**. Coat**s** are over there.
[z]	I'm looking for **an umbrella**. Umbrella**s** are over there.
[ɪz]	I'm looking for **a dress**. Dress**es** are over there.

THIS/THAT/THESE/THOSE

Is **this** your umbrella?
That umbrella is brown.

Are **these** your boots?
Those boots are dirty.

ADJECTIVES

This is a **purple** jacket.
These are **green** gloves.

KEY VOCABULARY

CLOTHING

belt	jacket	skirt
blouse	jeans	sock
boots	mittens	sports jacket
bracelet	necklace	stocking
briefcase	pajamas	suit
coat	pants	sunglasses
dress	pocketbook	sweater
earring	purse	tie
glasses	raincoat	umbrella
glove	shirt	watch
hat	shoe	

COLORS

black	pink
blue	purple
brown	red
gold	silver
gray	white
green	yellow
orange	

Clothing, Colors, and Cultures

Blue and pink aren't children's clothing colors all around the world

The meanings of colors are sometimes very different in different cultures. For example, in some cultures, blue is a common clothing color for little boys, and pink is a common clothing color for little girls. In other cultures, other colors are common for boys and girls.

There are also different colors for special days in different cultures. For example, white is the traditional color of a wedding dress in some cultures, but other colors are traditional in other cultures.

For some people, white is a happy color. For others, it's a sad color. For some people, red is a beautiful and lucky color. For others, it's a very sad color.

What are the meanings of different colors in YOUR culture?

LISTENING

Attention, J-Mart Shoppers!

_c_	① jackets	**a.**	Aisle 1
___	② gloves	**b.**	Aisle 7
___	③ blouses	**c.**	Aisle 9
___	④ bracelets	**d.**	Aisle 11
___	⑤ ties	**e.**	Aisle 5

BUILD YOUR VOCABULARY!

Clothing

That's a very nice _____ .

■ bathrobe

■ tee shirt

■ scarf

■ wallet

■ ring

Those are very nice _____ .

■ sandals

■ slippers

■ sneakers

■ shorts

■ sweat pants

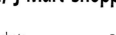

AROUND THE WORLD

People's Homes

Homes are different all around the world.

This family is living in a farmhouse.

This family is living in a hut.

This family is living in a houseboat.

These people are living in a mobile home (a trailer).

What different kinds of homes are there in your country?

FACT FILE

Urban, Suburban, and Rural

urban areas	=	cities
suburban areas	=	places near cities
rural areas	=	places in the countryside, far from cities

About 50% (percent) of the world's population is in urban and suburban areas.

About 50% (percent) of the world's population is in rural areas.

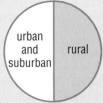

urban and suburban | rural

Global Exchange

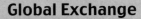

RosieM: My apartment is in a wonderful neighborhood. There's a big, beautiful park across from my apartment building. Around the corner, there's a bank, a post office, and a laundromat. There are also many restaurants and stores in my neighborhood. It's a noisy place, but it's a very interesting place. There are a lot of people on the sidewalks all day and all night. How about your neighborhood? Tell me about it.

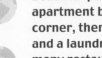

Send a message to a keypal. Tell about your neighborhood.

What Are They Saying?

Listening Scripts

Chapter 1 – Page 5

Listen and choose the correct answer.

1. A. What's your name?
   B. Mary Black.
2. A. What's your address?
   B. Two sixty-five Main Street.
3. A. What's your apartment number?
   B. Five C.
4. A. What's your telephone number?
   B. Two five nine – four oh eight seven.
5. A. What's your social security number?
   B. Oh three two – eight nine – six one seven nine.
6. A. What's your e-mail address?
   B. maryb-at-worldnet-dot-com.

Chapter 2 – Page 15

What's the Word?

Listen and choose the correct answer.

1. Mr. and Mrs. Lee are in the park.
2. Jim is in the hospital.
3. She's in the living room.
4. He's in the kitchen.
5. They're in the basement.
6. We're in the yard.

Where Are They?

Listen and choose the correct place.

1. A. Where's David?
   B. He's in the living room.
2. A. Where's Patty?
   B. She's in the bedroom.
3. A. Where are Mr. and Mrs. Kim?
   B. They're in the yard.
4. A. Where are you?
   B. I'm in the bathroom.
5. A. Where's the telephone book?
   B. It's in the kitchen.
6. A. Where are you and John?
   B. We're in the basement.

Chapter 3 – Page 23

Listen and choose the correct answer.

1. What are you doing?
2. What's Mr. Carter doing?
3. What's Ms. Miller doing?
4. What are Jim and Jane doing?
5. What are you and Peter doing?
6. What am I doing?

Side by Side Gazette – Page 26

Listen to the messages on Bob's machine. Match the messages.

You have seven messages.

Message Number One: "Hello. I'm calling for Robert White. This is Henry Drake. Mr. White, please call me at 427-9168. That's 427-9168. Thank you." [*beep*]

Message Number Two: "Hi, Bob! It's Patty. How are you? Call me!" [*beep*]

Message Number Three: "Bob? Hi. This is Kevin Carter from your guitar class. My phone number is 298-4577." [*beep*]

Message Number Four: "Mr. White? This is Linda Lee, from the social security office. Please call me. My telephone number is 969-0159." [*beep*]

Message Number Five: "Hello, Bob? This is Jim. I'm in the park. We're playing baseball. Call me, okay? My cell phone number is 682-4630." [*beep*]

Message Number Six: "Hello. Mr. White? This is Mrs. Lane on River Street. Your dog is in my yard. Call me at 731-0248." [*beep*]

Message Number Seven: "Hello, Bob. This is Dad. I'm at home. I'm reading the newspaper. Mom is planting flowers in the yard. It's a beautiful day. Where are you? What are you doing? Call us." [*beep*]

Chapter 4 – Page 33

Listen and choose the correct answer.

1. What are you eating?
2. What is she reading?
3. What is he playing?
4. What are they painting?
5. What are you watching?
6. What is he washing?

Chapter 5 – Page 43

What's the Answer?

Listen and choose the correct answer.

1. Tell me about your apartment.
2. Tell me about your new car.
3. Tell me about your neighbors.
4. How's the weather?
5. Tell me about your hotel.
6. How's the food at the restaurant?

True or False?

Listen to the conversation. Then answer True or False.

A. Hello.
B. Hello. Is this Betty?
A. Yes, it is.
B. Hi, Betty. This is Louise. I'm calling from Mud Beach.
A. From Mud Beach?
B. Yes. I'm on vacation in Mud Beach for a few days.
A. How's the weather in Mud Beach?
B. It's terrible! It's cold, and it's cloudy.
A. Cold and cloudy? What a shame! How's the hotel?
B. The hotel is terrible! It's old, it's noisy, and the rooms are very small.
A. I'm sorry to hear that. Tell me about the restaurants.
B. The restaurants in Mud Beach are expensive, and the food isn't very good. In fact, I'm having problems with my stomach.
A. What a shame! So, Louise, what are you doing?
B. I'm sitting in my room, and I'm watching TV. I'm not having a very good time.
A. I'm sorry to hear that.

Chapter 6 – Page 51

Quiet or Noisy?

Listen to the sentence. Are the people quiet or noisy?

1. He's listening to loud music.
2. She's reading.
3. He's sleeping.
4. The band is playing.
5. Everybody is singing and dancing.
6. He's studying.

What Do You Hear?

Listen to the sound. What do you hear? Choose the correct answer.

1. [Sound: singing]
2. [Sound: crying]
3. [Sound: vacuuming]
4. [Sound: laughing]
5. [Sound: drums]

Side by Side Gazette – Page 54

Listen to the weather reports. Match the weather and the cities.

This is Robby T. with the weather report from WXBC. It's a hot day in Honolulu today. The temperature here is one hundred degrees, and everybody is swimming at the beach.

This is Annie Lu with the weather report from WCLD in Atlanta. It's snowing here in Atlanta today, and everybody is at home.

This is Herbie Ross with today's weather from KFTG radio. It's warm and sunny here in Los Angeles today. The temperature is seventy degrees. It's a beautiful day.

This is Jimmy G. with your weather on CHME radio. It's cool and sunny here in Toronto today. It's a very nice day.

This is Lisa Lee with your WQRZ weather report. It's cold and cloudy in Chicago today. The temperature here is thirty-two degrees. Yes, it's a cold and cloudy day!

Chapter 7 – Page 65

What Places Do You Hear?

Listen and choose the correct places.

Ex.: My neighborhood is very nice. There's a supermarket across the street, and there's a video store around the corner.

1. My neighborhood is very convenient. There's a bank around the corner and a laundromat across the street.
2. My neighborhood is very noisy. There's a fire station next to my building, and there's a gas station across the street.
3. The sidewalks in my neighborhood are very busy. There's a school across the street and a department store around the corner.
4. There are many small stores in the center of my town. There's a bakery, a drug store, and a book store.
5. My neighborhood is very busy. There's a hotel across the street, and the hotel is between a hospital and a health club.

True or False?

Listen to the conversation. Then answer True or False.

A. Tell me about the apartment.
B. There's a large living room, a large kitchen, a nice bathroom, and a very nice bedroom.
A. How many closets are there in the apartment?
B. There's a closet in the bedroom and a closet in the living room.
A. Oh, I see. And how many windows are there in the living room?
B. There are four windows in the living room.
A. Four windows?
B. Yes. That's right.
A. Tell me. Is there a superintendent in the building?
B. Yes, there is.
A. And are there washing machines in the basement?
B. Yes, there are. There are three washing machines.
A. Oh, good. Tell me, is there an elevator in the building?
B. No, there isn't. But there's a fire escape.

Chapter 8 – Page 75

What's the Word?

Listen and choose the correct answer.

1. A. May I help you?
   B. Yes, please. I'm looking for a blouse.
2. A. Can I help you?
   B. Yes, please. I'm looking for a pair of boots.
3. A. May I help you?
   B. Yes, please. I'm looking for a necklace.
4. A. Can I help you?
   B. Yes, please. I'm looking for a raincoat.
5. A. May I help you?
   B. Yes, please. I'm looking for a pair of stockings.
6. A. Can I help you?
   B. Yes, please. I'm looking for a shirt.

Which Word Do You Hear?

Listen and choose the correct answer.

1. These jackets are expensive.
2. I'm looking for a leather belt.
3. I'm wearing my new wool sweater.
4. Suits are over there.
5. Is this your shoe?
6. Polka dot ties are very popular this year.

Side by Side Gazette – Page 77

Listen to these announcements in a clothing store. Match the clothing and the aisles.

Attention, J-Mart Shoppers! Are you looking for a black leather jacket? Black leather jackets are very popular this year! There are a lot of black leather jackets at J-Mart today! They're in Aisle 9, next to the coats.

Attention, J-Mart Shoppers! Are you looking for a pair of vinyl gloves? Vinyl gloves are very popular this year! Well, there are a lot of vinyl gloves at J-Mart today! They're in Aisle 5, across from the hats.

Attention, J-Mart Shoppers! Are you looking for a blouse? Is red your favorite color? Red blouses are very popular this year! There are a lot of red blouses at J-Mart today. They're in Aisle 7, next to the dresses.

Attention, J-Mart Shoppers! Are you looking for a special gift for your mother, your wife, or your sister? A silver bracelet is a special gift for that special person. All our silver bracelets are in Aisle 1, across from the earrings.

Attention, J-Mart Shoppers! Are you looking for a special gift for your father, your husband, or your brother? A polka dot tie is a special gift for that special person. All our polka dot ties are in Aisle 11, next to the belts.

Thematic Glossary

Classroom Objects

board 8
book 7
bookshelf 8
bulletin board 8
chair 8
clock 8
computer 7
desk 7
dictionary 8
globe 8
map 8
notebook 8
pen 7
pencil 7
ruler 8
table 8
wall 8

Clothing

bathrobe 77
belt 67
blouse 67
boot 68
bracelet 68
briefcase 68
coat 67
dress 67
earring 68
glasses 68
glove 68
hat 68
jacket 67
jeans 67
mitten 68
necklace 68
pajamas 67
pants 67
pocketbook 68
purse 68
raincoat 75
ring 77
sandals 77
scarf 77
shirt 67
shoe 67

shorts 77
skirt 67
slippers 77
sneakers 77
sock 67
sports jacket 72
stocking 68
suit 67
sunglasses 73
sweat pants 77
sweater 67
tee shirt 77
tie 67
umbrella 68
wallet 77
watch 68

Colors 70

black
blue
brown
gold
gray
green
orange
pink
purple
red
silver
white
yellow

Describing Feelings and Emotions

angry 49
cold 40
happy 22
hot 40
sad 77
tired 49

Describing People and Things

beautiful 22
big 35

busy 29
cheap 35
clean 72
difficult 35
dirty 72
easy 35
empty 72
expensive 35
fat 35
frustrated 75
good 42
handsome 35
happy 22
heavy 35
inexpensive 75
interesting 13
large 35
little 35
loud 35
married 35
new 35
noisy 35
old 35
poor 35
pretty 35
quiet 35
rich 35
sad 77
short 35
single 35
small 35
tall 35
thin 35
ugly 35
young 35

Everyday Activities

act 48
bake 47
brush *their* teeth 27
clean 27
cook 17
cry 47
dance 48
do *our* exercises 30
do *their* homework 28

drink 17
eat 17
feed 27
fix 27
have *dinner* 46
laugh 50
listen to 17
paint 27
plant 17
play *baseball* 17
play *cards* 17
play the *piano* 17
read 17
ride 46
shop 63
sing 17
skateboard 47
sleep 17
study 17
swim 17
talk 50
teach 17
use 53
vacuum 49
wash 27
watch TV 17
write 42

Family Members

aunt 45
brother 45
brother-in-law 54
children 45
cousin 45
daughter 45
daughter-in-law 54
father 45
father-in-law 54
grandchildren 45
granddaughter 45
grandfather 45
grandmother 45
grandparents 45
grandson 45
husband 45
mother 45
mother-in-law 54
nephew 45

niece 45
parents 45
sister 45
sister-in-law 54
son 45
son-in-law 54
uncle 45
wife 45

Personal Information

address 1
apartment number 4
e-mail address 4
fax number 4
first name 4
last name 4
name 1
phone number 1
telephone number 1

Places Around Town

airport 63
bakery 55
bank 7
barber shop 55
book store 55
bus station 55
cafeteria 21
church 21
clinic 37
clothing store 63
department store 55
drug store 55
fire station 56
gas station 56
hair salon 55
health club 31
hospital 14
hotel 42
laundromat 31
library 7
movie theater 14
park 14
police station 57
post office 7
restaurant 7

school 55
shopping mall 63
supermarket 7
train station 55
video store 55
zoo 14

Places at Home

attic 10
basement 10
bathroom 7
bedroom 7
dining room 7
garage 10
kitchen 7
living room 7
yard 10

Skills

act 48
bake 47
cook 17
dance 48
fix 27
paint 27
sing 17
talk 50
teach 17

Time Expressions

day 22
night 49
year 70

Weather 40

cloudy
cold
cool
hot
rain
snow
sunny
warm

Cardinal Numbers

1	one	20	twenty	
2	two	21	twenty-one	
3	three	22	twenty-two	
4	four	.	.	
5	five	.	.	
6	six	29	twenty-nine	
7	seven	30	thirty	
8	eight	40	forty	
9	nine	50	fifty	
10	ten	60	sixty	
11	eleven	70	seventy	
12	twelve	80	eighty	
13	thirteen	90	ninety	
14	fourteen	100	one hundred	
15	fifteen	200	two hundred	
16	sixteen	.	.	
17	seventeen	900	nine hundred	
18	eighteen	1,000	one thousand	
19	nineteen	2,000	two thousand	
		10,000	ten thousand	
		100,000	one hundred thousand	
		1,000,000	one million	

Index

ACTIVITY WORKBOOK

SIDE by SIDE

THIRD EDITION

BOOK 1A

Steven J. Molinsky
Bill Bliss

with

Carolyn Graham • Peter S. Bliss

Contributing Authors

Dorothy Lynde • Elizabeth Handley

Illustrated by
Richard E. Hill

CONTENTS

Listening Scripts

Page 3 Exercise C

Listen and circle the number you hear.

1. My address is five Main Street.
2. My address is seven Main Street.
3. My address is two Main Street.
4. My address is six Main Street.
5. My address is one Main Street.
6. My address is three Main Street.
7. My address is four Main Street.
8. My address is eight Main Street.
9. My address is ten Main Street.
10. My address is nine Main Street.

Page 4 Exercise E

Listen and write the missing numbers.

1. A. What's your phone number?
   B. My phone number is 389-7932.
2. A. What's your telephone number?
   B. My telephone number is 837-2953.
3. A. What's your apartment number?
   B. My apartment number is 6-B.
4. A. What's your address?
   B. My address is 10 Main Street.
5. A. What's your fax number?
   B. My fax number is 654-7315.
6. A. What's your license number?
   B. My license number is 2613498.

Page 5 Exercise F

Listen and write the missing letters.

1. A. What's your last name?
   B. Carter.
   A. How do you spell that?
   B. C-A-R-T-E-R.
2. A. What's your last name?
   B. Johnson.
   A. How do you spell that?
   B. J-O-H-N-S-O-N.
3. A. What's your first name?
   B. Gerald.
   A. How do you spell that?
   B. G-E-R-A-L-D.
4. A. What's your last name?
   B. Anderson.
   A. How do you spell that?
   B. A-N-D-E-R-S-O-N.
5. A. What's your first name?
   B. Phillip.
   A. How do you spell that?
   B. P-H-I-L-L-I-P.
6. A. What's your last name?
   B. Martinez.
   A. How do you spell that?
   B. M-A-R-T-I-N-E-Z.

Page 6 Exercise B

Listen and put a check under the correct picture.

1. A. Where's the book?
   B. It's on the desk.
2. A. Where's the dictionary?
   B. It's on the chair.
3. A. Where's the ruler?
   B. It's on the desk.
4. A. Where's the map?
   B. It's on the bulletin board.
5. A. Where's the globe?
   B. It's on the bookshelf.
6. A. Where's the computer?
   B. It's on the table.

Page 11 Exercise J

Listen and write the number under the correct picture.

1. Our English teacher is in the hospital.
2. Mr. and Mrs. Sanchez are in the restaurant.
3. Mary is at the dentist.
4. Billy and Jimmy are in the park.
5. Mr. and Mrs. Lee are at the social security office.
6. James is home in bed.

Page 11 Exercise K

Listen and circle the word you hear.

1. Where are you?
2. Ms. Jones is in the bank.
3. We're friends.
4. Hi. How are you?
5. Where's the newspaper?
6. He's from Korea.
7. The computer is on the table.
8. It's in the bathroom.

Page 15 Exercise C

Listen and put a check under the correct picture.

1. He's eating lunch.
2. We're drinking milk.
3. I'm playing the guitar.
4. She's playing the piano.
5. We're cooking breakfast.
6. It's in the classroom.
7. I'm reading.
8. He's watching TV.
9. She's studying mathematics.
10. They're playing baseball in the yard.

Page 20 Exercise D

Listen and write the letter or number you hear.

Ex. A. What's your first name?
    B. Mark.
    A. How do you spell that?
    B. M-A-R-K.

1. A. What's your last name?
   B. Carter.
   A. How do you spell that?
   B. C-A-R-T-E-R.
2. A. What's your telephone number?
   B. My telephone number is 354-9812.
3. A. What's your fax number?
   B. My fax number is 890-7462.
4. A. What's your first name?
   B. Julie.
   A. How do you spell that?
   B. J-U-L-I-E.
5. A. What's your telephone number?
   B. My telephone number is 672-3059.

6. A. What's your license number?
   B. My license number is 5170349.

Page 22 Exercise C

Listen and circle the word you hear.

1. We're cleaning our room.
2. He's doing his homework.
3. She's washing her hair.
4. They're fixing their car.
5. You're fixing your TV.
6. I'm feeding my cat.

Page 24 Exercise G

Listen and circle the word you hear.

1. He's studying.
2. She's doing her homework.
3. I'm feeding my cat.
4. He's cleaning his yard.
5. We're fixing our car.
6. They're washing their clothes.

Page 27 Exercise C

Listen and circle the word you hear.

1. Sally's brother is very tall.
2. Their dog is very heavy.
3. The questions in my English book are very easy.
4. My friend George is single.
5. Mary's cat is very ugly!
6. This book is very cheap.

Page 32 Exercise K

Listen and circle the word you hear.

1. A. How's the weather in Rome today?
   B. It's cool.
2. A. How's the weather in Tokyo today?
   B. It's snowing.
3. A. How's the weather in Seoul today?
   B. It's sunny.
4. A. How's the weather in Shanghai today?
   B. It's hot.
5. A. How's the weather in New York today?
   B. It's raining.
6. A. How's the weather in Miami today?
   B. It's cloudy.

Page 34 Exercise O

Listen to the temperature in Fahrenheit and Celsius. Write the numbers you hear.

1. In Los Angeles, it's 86° Fahrenheit/30° Celsius.
2. In Seoul, it's 32° Fahrenheit/0° Celsius.
3. In San Juan, it's 81° Fahrenheit/27° Celsius.
4. In Hong Kong, it's 72° Fahrenheit/22° Celsius.
5. In Miami, it's 93° Fahrenheit/34° Celsius.
6. In London, it's 56° Fahrenheit/13° Celsius.
7. In Mexico City, it's 66° Fahrenheit/19° Celsius.
8. In Moscow, it's 34° Fahrenheit/1° Celsius.

Page 36 Exercise B

Listen and put a check under the correct picture.

1. In this photograph, my sister is skateboarding in the park.
2. In this photograph, my son is acting in a play.
3. In this photograph, my friends are dancing at my wedding.
4. In this photograph, my uncle is baking a cake.

5. In this photograph, my cousin is playing a game on her computer.
6. In this photograph, my husband is standing in front of our apartment building.
7. In this photograph, my grandparents are having dinner.
8. In this photograph, my aunt is planting flowers.

Page 40 Exercise E

Listen and choose the correct response.

Ex. Is he old?

1. Is it large?
2. Is she poor?
3. Is it sunny?
4. Is he quiet?

Page 43 Exercise C

Listen to the sentences about the buildings on the map. After each sentence, write the name on the correct building.

1. There's a bakery between the barber shop and the bank.
2. There's a school next to the church.
3. There's a department store across from the school and the church.
4. There's a library around the corner from the barber shop.
5. There's a hospital across from the library.
6. There's a police station next to the hospital.
7. There's a hair salon across from the barber shop.
8. There's a supermarket next to the hair salon.
9. There's a video store around the corner from the bank.
10. There's a park between the library and the video store.
11. There's a health club around the corner from the department store.
12. There's a train station across from the health club.

Page 51 Exercise D

Listen and circle the word you hear.

1. umbrellas
2. blouses
3. coats
4. computer
5. shoes
6. exercises
7. dress
8. restaurants
9. necklaces
10. earring
11. belt
12. watches
13. nieces
14. nephew
15. shirts
16. tie

Page 52 Exercise E

Listen and circle the color you hear.

1. My favorite color is blue.
2. My favorite color is green.
3. My favorite color is gray.
4. My favorite color is silver.
5. My favorite color is yellow.
6. My favorite color is orange.

Page 54 Exercise H

Listen and put a check under the correct picture.

1. I'm washing these socks.
2. He's reading this book.
3. I'm looking for these men.
4. They're using these computers.
5. We're vacuuming this rug.
6. She's playing with these dogs.
7. We're painting this garage.
8. They're listening to these radios.

Page 54 Exercise I

Listen and circle the correct word to complete the sentence.

1. This bicycle . . .
2. These exercises . . .
3. These apartment buildings . . .
4. This bracelet . . .
5. These women . . .
6. These sunglasses . . .
7. This car . . .
8. These jeans . . .
9. This refrigerator . . .

Page 61 Exercise F

Listen and circle the correct word to complete the sentence.

Ex. These dresses . . .

1. That house . . .
2. Those people . . .
3. These flowers . . .
4. This blouse . . .

WHAT ARE THEY SAYING?

what's	is	my	from	name	phone number
where	are	your	I'm	address	

1. _____What's_____ your name?

My _____ is Janet Miller.

2. What's your _____?

_____ address _____ 456 Main Street.

3. What's _____ phone number?

My _____ _____ is 654-3960.

4. What's _____ name?

My _____ is Ken Green.

5. _____ your address?

My _____ is 15 Park Street.

6. What's your _____ number?

_____ phone _____ is 379-1029.

7. _____ _____ you from?

_____ _____ Detroit.

B NAME/ADDRESS/PHONE NUMBER

STUDENT IDENTIFICATION CARD

Name: ___Maria___   ___Gonzalez___
          First Name   Last Name

Address: ___235 Main Street___

          ___Bronx, New York___

Phone
Number: ___741-8906___

My name is Maria Gonzalez.
My address is 235 Main Street.
My phone number is 741-8906.

How about you? What's YOUR name, address, and phone number?

STUDENT IDENTIFICATION CARD

Name: _____
        First Name   Last Name

Address: _____

          _____

Phone
Number: _____

My name _____ ....

....

My _____ _____ ....

....

My _____ _____ _____ _____

....

C LISTENING

Listen and circle the number you hear.

1. (5) / 9

2. 3 / 7

3. 1 / 2

4. 6 / 3

5. 4 / 1

6. 3 / 6

7. 5 / 4

8. 8 / 2

9. 10 / 0

10. 5 / 9

D NUMBERS

zero	0
one	1
two	2
three	3
four	4
five	5
six	6
seven	7
eight	8
nine	9
ten	10

Write the number.

four _____4_____

seven _____

one _____

eight _____

ten _____

two _____

nine _____

six _____

five _____

three _____

Write the word.

6 _____six_____

2 _____

7 _____

3 _____

1 _____

8 _____

10 _____

4 _____

9 _____

5 _____

E LISTENING

Listen and write the missing numbers.

1.
What's your phone number?
My phone number is 389-793_2_.

2.
What's your telephone number?
My telephone number is 837-29___3.

3.
What's your apartment number?
My apartment number is ___-B.

4.
What's your address?
My address is ___ Main Street.

5.
What's your fax number?
My fax number is 654-___ ___15.

6.
What's your license number?
My license number is 26___3___9___.

4   Activity Workbook

Listen and write the missing letters.

1. C-A-_R_-T-___-R

2. J-O-___-N-___-O-___

3. ___-E-R-___-L-___

4. A-N-D-E-___-S-___-N

5. ___-H-I-L-___-I-P

6. ___-A-R-___-I-N-E-___

G **WHAT ARE THEY SAYING?**

name	meet	you	Hi	Nice

A. Hello. My ___name___¹ is Dan Harris.

B. _____². I'm Susan Wilson.

Nice to _____³ you.

A. _____⁴ to meet _____⁵, too.

is	you	Hello	I'm	My	to

A. Hi. _____⁶ name _____⁷ Alice Lane.

B. _____⁸. _____⁹ Bob Chang.

A. Nice _____¹⁰ meet you.

B. Nice to meet _____¹¹, too.

H **GRAMMARRAP:** *Hi! Hello!*

Listen. Then clap and practice.

A. Hi. I'm Jack.

B. Hello. I'm Jill.

C. Hi. I'm Mary.

D. Hello. I'm Bill.

All. Nice to meet you.

Nice to meet you, too.

A. Hi. I'm Bob.

B. Hello. I'm Tim.

C. Hi. I'm Susie.

D. Hello. I'm Jim.

All. Nice to meet you.

Nice to meet you, too.

 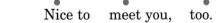

Across

1.   5.

6.   8.

10.   12.

Down

1.   2.

3.   4.   7.

8.   9.   11.

D I C T I O N A R Y

B **LISTENING**

Listen and put a check (✓) under the correct picture.

1. __✔__ _____   2. _____ _____   3. _____ _____

4. _____ _____   5. _____ _____   6. _____ _____

WHAT ARE THEY SAYING?

I'm	are	basement	attic	living room
we're	where	dining room	yard	bedroom
they're	you	kitchen	bathroom	

1. _____Where_____ are you?

  __I'm__ in the _____.

2. Where _____ Susan and Joe?

  _____ in the _____.

3. Where _____ you and Julie?

  _____ in the _____.

4. _____ are you?

  _____ in the _____.

5. _____ _____ Ben and Maria?

  _____ in the _____.

6. Where _____ you and Betty?

  _____ in the _____.

7. _____ _____ Pam and Peter?

  _____ in the _____.

8. _____ _____ you?

  _____ in the _____.

Activity Workbook 7

D WHAT ARE THEY SAYING?

where's	she's	classroom	garage	he's	living room	it's

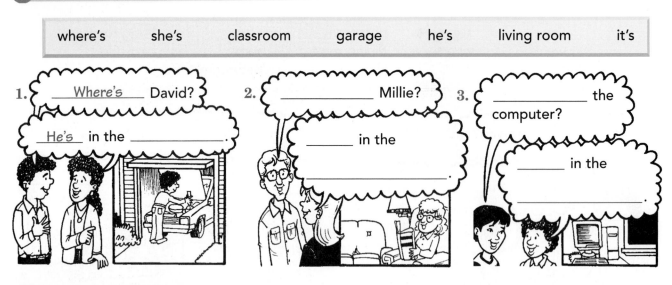

1. __Where's__ David?

__He's__ in the _____.

2. _____ Millie?

_____ in the _____.

3. _____ the computer?

_____ in the _____.

E WHERE ARE THEY?

	(Mr. and Mrs. Chen)	1. _____They_____ are in the kitchen.
	(Ms. Carter)	2. _____ is in the dining room.
	(Mr. Grant)	3. _____ is in the bathroom.
	(Harry and Mary)	4. _____ are in the basement.
we he they	(Ellen and I)	5. _____ are in the attic.
she	(The bookshelf)	6. _____ is in the living room.
it	(Mr. White)	7. _____ is in the garage.
	(Mrs. Miller)	8. _____ is in the classroom.
	(The telephone book)	9. _____ is in the bedroom.

F WHERE ARE THEY?

	(He is)	1. _____He's_____ in the bedroom.
	(They are)	2. _____ in the basement.
	(We are)	3. _____ in the attic.
I'm we're he's where's	(I am)	4. _____ in the bathroom.
you're she's	(It is)	5. _____ in the dining room.
they're it's	(She is)	6. _____ in the living room.
	(You are)	7. _____ in the garage.
	(Where is)	8. _____ the cell phone?

G THE BAKER FAMILY

The Baker family is at home today. (1) Mrs. Baker is ___in___ ___the___ ___living___
___room___. (2) Mr. Baker is _____ _____ _____. (3) Peggy and Jim are _____
_____ _____. (4) Kevin is _____ _____ _____. (5) Susie is _____ _____
_____. (6) And the car is _____ _____ _____.

H WHERE ARE THEY?

he's	they're
she's	
it's	

1. Where's Mrs. Baker?   _She's in the living room._____

2. Where's Mr. Baker?   _____

3. Where are Peggy and Jim?   _____

4. Where's Kevin?   _____

5. Where's Susie?   _____

6. Where's the car?   _____

1 WHAT'S THE SIGN?

Fill in the signs. Then complete the sentences.

1. Helen is _____*in the park*_____.

2. Mr. and Mrs. Grant are _____ _____.

3. Edward is _____.

4. Maria is _____.

5. Jim and Sarah are _____ _____.

6. Billy is _____.

7. The monkey is _____.

8. Ms. Johnson is _____.

Listen and write the number under the correct picture.

1

K **LISTENING**

Listen and circle the word you hear.

1.	zoo	(you)	3.	We're	They're	5.	Where	Where's	7.	on	in
2.	Ms.	Mr.	4.	Where	How	6.	She's	He's	8.	Is	It's

L **MATCHING**

Match the nationality and the city.

_c_ 1. We're Mexican. We're from _____.   a. Shanghai

____ 2. She's Greek. She's from _____.   b. San Juan

____ 3. He's Chinese. He's from _____.   c. Mexico City

____ 4. I'm Italian. I'm from_____.   d. Seoul

____ 5. They're Puerto Rican. They're from _____. e. Athens

____ 6. We're Korean. We're from _____.   f. Tokyo

____ 7. She's Japanese. She's from _____.   g. Rome

M GRAMMARRAP: *Where's Jack?*

Listen. Then clap and practice.

A. Where's   Jack?

B. He's in the   kitchen.

A. Where's   Jill?

B. She's in the   dining room.

A. Where's   Mom?

B. She's in the   living room.

A. Where's   Fred?   Fred's in   bed.

All. Fred's in   bed.

Fred's in   bed.

A. Jack's in the kitchen.

All. Fred's in   bed.

A. Jack's in the kitchen.

B. Jill's in the dining room.

A. Mom's in the   living room.

All. Fred's in   bed.

N GRAMMARRAP: *Where Are Fred and Mary?*

Listen. Then clap and practice.

Where are	Fred and Mary

A. Where's Jack?   A. Jack and   Jill.

B. Where's Jill?   B. Betty and   Bill.

C. Where are Fred and Mary?   C. Bob and   Lou.

D. Where's Bill?   D. Mary and   Sue.

A. Where's Ed?   A. Jack and   Jill.

B. Where's Sue?   B. Betty and   Bill.

C. Where are Bob and   Betty?   C. Bob and   Lou.

D. Where are Tom and Lou?   D. Mary and   Sue.

A WHAT ARE THEY SAYING?

doing	watching	I'm	we're	you
reading	sleeping	he's	they're	what
playing	eating	she's	are	what's
studying	cooking			

1. _____What_____ are you doing?

   I'm _____ English.

2. What's Carla _____?

   _____.

3. _____ Walter doing?

   _____.

4. _____ _____ Julie and David doing?

   _____ the newspaper.

5. _____ _____ you and George doing?

   _____ _____ TV.

6. _____ you _____?

   _____ _____ the piano.

7. _____ William doing?

   _____ dinner.

Activity Workbook   **13**

cooking	eating	playing	singing	studying	watching
drinking	listening	reading	sleeping	teaching	

1. He's _____eating_____ breakfast.

2. She's _____ milk.

3. They're _____ mathematics.

4. He's _____ the newspaper.

5. They're _____.

6. She's _____.

7. He's _____ to music.

8. They're _____ TV.

9. She's _____ dinner.

10. He's _____.

11. They're _____ baseball.

Listen and put a check (✓) under the correct picture.

1. _____ ✔ _____   _____   2. _____   _____

3. _____   _____   4. _____   _____

5. _____   _____   6. _____   _____

7. _____   _____   8. _____   _____

9. _____   _____   10. _____   _____

D GRAMMARRAP: *Frank?! At the Bank?!*

Listen. Then clap and practice.

A. Where's   Frank?

B. He's working at the   bank.

A. Frank?!   At the bank?!

B. Yes, that's   right.

He's working at the   bank.

All. Frank?!   At the bank?!   Oh,   no!

A. Where's   Sue?

B. She's working at the   zoo.

A. Sue?!   At the zoo?!

B. Yes, that's   right.

She's working at the   zoo.

All. Sue?!   At the zoo?!   Oh,   no!

A. Where's   Paul?

B. He's working at the   mall.

A. Paul?!   At the mall?!

B. Yes, that's   right.

He's working at the   mall.

All. Paul?!   At the mall?!   Oh,   no!

E WHAT'S THE QUESTION?

| Where is | he / she / it | ? | What's | he / she / it | doing? |
| Where are | you / they | ? | What are | you / they | doing? |

1. ___Where___ ___are___ ___you___ ?

      I'm in the garage

2. ___What's___ ___he___ ___doing___ ?

      He's cooking dinner.

3. _____ _____ _____ ?

      They're in the park.

4. _____ ?

      We're playing with the dog.

5. _____ _____ _____ ?

      He's in the attic.

6. _____ ?

      She's listening to the radio.

7. _____ _____ _____ ?

      She's in the yard.

8. _____ ?

      We're at the beach.

9. _____ ?

      He's sleeping.

10. _____ _____ ?

      It's in the classroom.

11. _____ ?

      They're eating lunch.

12. _____ _____ _____ ?

      I'm in the hospital.

Listen. Then clap and practice.

What's he	Where are	What are

A. Where's   Charlie?

B. He's in the   kitchen.

A. What's he   doing?

B. Eating   lunch.

All. Charlie's in the   kitchen   eating   lunch.

   Charlie's in the   kitchen   eating   lunch.

A. Who's in the   kitchen?

B. Charlie's in the kitchen.

A. What's he   doing?

B. Eating   lunch.

A. Where's   Betty?

B. She's in the   bedroom.

A. What's she   doing?

B. Reading a   book.

All. Betty's in the bedroom reading a book.

Betty's in the bedroom reading a book.

A. Who's in the bedroom?

B. Betty's in the bedroom.

A. What's she doing?

B. Reading a book.

A. Where are Mom and Dad?

B. They're in the living room.

A. What are they doing?

B. Watching Channel Seven.

All. Betty's in the bedroom.

Mom's in the living room.

Dad's in the living room.

Charlie's in the kitchen.

A. Where's Charlie?

All. He's in the kitchen.

A. What's he doing?

All. Eating lunch.

✓ CHECK-UP TEST: Chapters 1-3

A. Answer the questions.

Ex. What's your telephone number?

My .....telephone number is 567-1032.

1. What's your name?

....

2. What's your address?

....

3. Where are you from?

....

B. Circle the correct answer.

Ex. The map is on the | yard / (wall) / park |.

1. We're eating | milk / cards / lunch |.

2. | What / Where's / What's | Ben doing?

3. Max is | planting flowers / swimming / singing | in the bathroom.

4. Ms. Park is teaching | dinner / mathematics / the radio |.

5. Nice to | hello / hi / meet | you.

6. The | pencil / attic / shower | is in the classroom.

C. Fill in the blanks.

Ex. ___What's___ Bill doing?

1. Maria is _____ the hospital.

2. I'm _____ the newspaper.

3. Where's Joe? _____ in the cafeteria.

4. They're _____ TV.

5. What are you and Peter doing? _____ reading.

6. _____ the car? It's in the garage.

7. What are you _____? I'm studying.

8. Where's the cell phone? _____ in the basement.

9. _____ are Mr. and Mrs. Chen doing?

10. Carol _____ Bob are eating breakfast.

D. Listen and write the letter or number you hear.

Ex. M-A-R- K

1. C-A-R-___E-R

2. 354-9___12

3. 890-74___2

4. ___-U-L-I-E

5. 6___2-3059

6. 517___349

what	my	our	cleaning	apartment
what's	his	their	doing	children
are	her		fixing	homework
				sink

1. Hi! ___What's___ Jason doing?

   He's _____

   _____ room.

2. What's Peggy _____?

   She's _____

   _____ car.

3. _____ are you doing?

   I'm cleaning _____

   _____.

4. What are your _____ doing?

   They're doing _____

   _____.

5. What _____ you doing?   We're fixing _____ _____.

B WHAT'S THE WORD?

my	his	her	its	our	your	their

1. I'm feeding _____my_____ cat.

2. We're washing _____ clothes.

3. They're painting _____ bedroom.

4. She's fixing _____ sink.

5. It's eating _____ dinner.

6. You're cleaning _____ yard.

7. He's reading _____ e-mail.

C LISTENING

Listen and circle the word you hear.

1. your   (our)   3. her   his   5. your   our

2. his   her   4. our   their   6. my   its

D PUZZLE

Across

1. I'm painting _____ apartment.

3. We're fixing _____ TV.

6. Bobby and Tim are cleaning _____ room.

7. Bill is doing _____ homework.

Down

2. You're doing _____ exercises.

4. The dog is eating _____ dinner.

5. Ruth is brushing _____ teeth.

| Yes, I am. | Yes, { he / she / it } is. | Yes, { we / you / they } are. |

1. A. Is Harry feeding his cat?

   B. <u>Yes, he is.</u>

2. A. Are you and Tom cleaning your yard?

   B. _____ _____ _____

3. A. Is Mrs. Chen doing her exercises?

   B. _____ _____ _____

4. A. Are your children brushing their teeth?

   B. _____ _____ _____

5. A. Is George sleeping?

   B. _____ _____ _____

6. A. Is Irene planting flowers?

   B. _____ _____ _____

7. A. Are you washing your windows?

   B. _____ _____ _____

8. A. Am I in the hospital?

   B. _____ _____ _____

F **GrammarRap:** *Busy! Busy! Busy!*

Listen. Then clap and practice.

What are	Is he	Yes, he	What's he

A.   Are you busy?

B.   Yes, I   am.

A.   What are you   doing?

B.   I'm talking to   Sam.

A.   Is he busy?

B.   Yes, he   is.

A.   What's he   doing?

B.   He's talking to   Liz.

A.   Are they busy?

B.   Yes, they   are.

A.   What are they   doing?

B.   They're washing their   car.

All.   I'm talking to   Sam.

          He's talking to   Liz.

     They're washing their   car.

        They're busy!

G **LISTENING**

Listen and circle the word you hear.

1. (he's)   she's   3. feeding   eating   5. our   their

2. his   her   4. apartment   yard   6. washing   watching

24   Activity Workbook

H WHAT ARE THEY DOING?

1. He's _____washing_____ his hair.

3. We're _____ our exercises.

5. She's _____ her living room.

2. They're _____ their yard.

4. I'm _____ my e-mail.

6. You're _____ your cat.

I WHAT'S THE WORD?

Circle the correct words.

1. (They're) / Their   washing   they're / their   windows.

2. Where / We're   are Mr. and Mrs. Tanaka?

3. He's / His   doing   he's / his   exercises.

4. Where are / Where's   the cell phone?

5. We're brushing   are / our   teeth.

6. His / Is   Richard busy?

7. What   are / our   you doing?

8. The cat is eating   it's / its   dinner.

Activity Workbook   25

laundromat	doing	playing	they're	what's	her	are
library	eating	reading	he's	where's	their	and
park	fixing	washing	she's	in	his
restaurant	listening				

Everybody is busy today. Ms. Roberts is in the ____restaurant____ ¹. She's _____ ²

dinner. Mr. and Mrs. Lopez are _____ ³ the health club. _____ ⁴ doing _____ ⁵

exercises. Patty and Danny Williams are in the _____ ⁶. She's _____ ⁷ the

newspaper. He's _____ ⁸ to music. Mr. _____ ⁹ Mrs. Sharp are also in the park.

What are they _____ ¹⁰? They're _____ ¹¹ cards.

Jenny Chang is in the _____ ¹². _____ ¹³ washing _____ ¹⁴ clothes.

Charlie Harris and Julie Carter _____ ¹⁵ in the parking lot. He's _____ ¹⁶

_____ ¹⁷ car. She's _____ ¹⁸ her bicycle. _____ ¹⁹ Mr. Molina? He's in the

_____ ²⁰. _____ ²¹ he doing? _____ ²² reading a book.

_d_	1.	large	a.	thin	___	8.	tall	h.	heavy
___	2.	heavy	b.	rich	___	9.	difficult	i.	old
___	3.	single	c.	beautiful	___	10.	new	j.	ugly
___	4.	ugly	d.	small	___	11.	handsome	k.	big
___	5.	cheap	e.	young	___	12.	thin	l.	easy
___	6.	poor	f.	expensive	___	13.	little	m.	noisy
___	7.	old	g.	married	___	14.	quiet	n.	short

B WHAT ARE THEY SAYING?

Tell me about your new friend.

1. Is he short or _____ tall _____ ?

2. Is he heavy or _____ ?

3. Is he old or _____ ?

4. Is he single or _____ ?

Tell me about the apartment.

5. Is it large or _____ ?

6. Is it quiet or _____ ?

7. Is it cheap or _____ ?

8. Is it beautiful or _____ ?

C LISTENING

Listen and circle the word you hear.

1. small (tall)   3. easy   noisy   5. ugly   young

2. ugly   heavy   4. thin   single   6. cheap   easy

Activity Workbook   **27**

D WHAT'S WRONG?

He She It } isn't	They aren't

1. It's new.

   ____It isn't new.____

   ____It's old.____

2. They're quiet.

   _____

   _____

3. It's large.

   _____

   _____

4. He's single.

   _____

   _____

5. She's young.

   _____

   _____

6. They're short.

   _____

   _____

E SCRAMBLED QUESTIONS

Unscramble the questions. Begin each question with a capital letter.

1. _____Are you busy_____?
   busy   you   are

2. _____?
   dog   your   large   is

3. _____?
   they   are   married

4. _____?
   I   beautiful   am

5. _____?
   difficult   English   is

6. _____?
   new   is   car   their

7. _____?
   tall   she   is   short   or

8. _____?
   noisy   quiet   he   is   or

F **GRAMMARRAP:** *Old! Cold! Tall! Small!*

Listen. Then clap and practice.

All.	Is he	young?	*(clap) (clap)*
	Is he	old?	*(clap) (clap)*
	Is it	hot?	*(clap) (clap)*
	Is it	cold?	*(clap) (clap)*
	Is she	short?	*(clap) (clap)*
	Is she	tall?	*(clap) (clap)*
	Is it	large?	*(clap) (clap)*
	Is it	small?	*(clap) (clap)*

Young!	Old!
Hot!	Cold!
Young!	Old!
Hot!	Cold!

A. Is he young or old?

B. He's very old.

A. Is it hot or cold?

B. It's very cold.

A. Is she short or tall?

B. She's very tall.

A. Is it large or small?

B. It's extremely small.

All.	Young!	Old!
	Hot!	Cold!
	Short!	Tall!
	Large!	Small!

| bicycle | book | car | cat | computer | dog | guitar | house | piano | TV |

1. _____Albert's_____ _____car_____

2. _____Jenny's_____ _____bicycle_____

3. _____ _____

4. _____ _____

5. _____ _____

6. _____ _____

7. _____ _____

8. _____ _____

9. _____ _____

10. _____ _____

H WHAT'S THE WORD?

His	Her	Their	Its

1. Mary's brother isn't short.   (His (Her)) brother is tall.

2. Mr. and Mrs. Miller's apartment isn't cheap.   (His   Their) apartment is expensive.

3. Robert's sister isn't single.   (His   Her) sister is married.

4. Ms. Clark's neighbors aren't quiet.   (Their   Her) neighbors are noisy.

5. Their dog's name isn't Rover.   (Its   Their) name is Fido.

6. Mrs. Hunter's car isn't large.   (His   Her) car is small.

7. Timmy's bicycle isn't new.   (His   Its) bicycle is old.

8. Mr. and Mrs. Lee's son isn't single.   (Her   Their) son is married.

I MR. AND MRS. GRANT

Read the story and answer the questions.

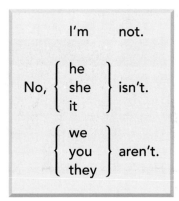

Meet Mr. and Mrs. Grant. Mr. Grant is short and heavy. Mrs. Grant is tall and thin. Their house is small and old. Their car is new and expensive. Their neighbors are noisy. And their cat is ugly.

1. Is Mr. Grant short?   _Yes, he is._   8. Is their house large?   _____

2. Is he tall?   _____   9. Is it old?   _____

3. Is he thin?   _____   10. Is their car new?   _____

4. Is he heavy?   _____   11. Is it cheap?   _____

5. Is Mrs. Grant tall?   _____   12. Are their neighbors quiet?   _____

6. Is she heavy?   _____   13. Are they noisy?   _____

7. Is she thin?   _____   14. Is their cat pretty?   _____

it's sunny	it's raining	it's warm	it's hot
it's cloudy	it's snowing	it's cool	it's cold

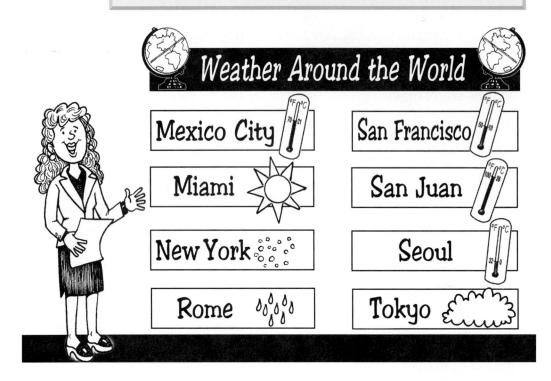

Weather Around the World

Mexico City
Miami
New York
Rome

San Francisco
San Juan
Seoul
Tokyo

1. How's the weather in Mexico City?   <u>It's</u> _____ <u>warm.</u>_____

2. How's the weather in Miami?   _____ _____

3. How's the weather in New York?   _____ _____

4. How's the weather in Rome?   _____ _____

5. How's the weather in San Francisco?   _____ _____

6. How's the weather in San Juan?   _____ _____

7. How's the weather in Seoul?   _____ _____

8. How's the weather in Tokyo?   _____ _____

9. How's the weather in YOUR city?   ....

K **LISTENING**

Listen and circle the word you hear.

1. cold   (cool)   3. sunny   snowing   5. raining   snowing

2. snowing   sunny   4. cool   hot   6. sunny   cloudy

D **GRAMMARSONG:** *Pictures on the Wall*

Listen and fill in the words to the song. Then listen again and sing along.

| crying | dancing | hanging | having | living | looking | smiling | working |

I'm looking at the photographs.

They're hanging in the hall.

I'm ___smiling___ 1 at the memories,

looking at the pictures on the wall.

My son Robert's married now.

I'm _____ 2 in L.A. (Hi, Dad!)

My daughter's _____ 3 in Detroit.

I'm very far away. (I love you, Dad!)

I'm _____ 4 at the photographs.

They're _____ 5 in the hall.

I'm smiling at the memories,

looking at the pictures on the wall.

My mom and dad are _____ 6.

It's a very special day.

(We're _____ 7 a good time!)

My little sister's _____ 8.

It's my brother's wedding day.
(I'm so happy!)

I'm _____ 9 at the photographs.

They're _____ 10 in the hall.

I'm _____ 11 at the memories,

_____ 12 at the pictures on the wall.

I'm smiling at the memories,

looking at the pictures on the wall.

Activity Workbook **37**

E AN E-MAIL FROM LOS ANGELES

```
To: alex@ttm.com
From: bob@aal.com

Dear Alex,

     Our new home in Los Angeles is large and pretty.  Los Angeles is
beautiful.  The weather is warm and sunny.  Today it's 78˚F.
     Our family is in the park today, and we're having a good time.  My
mother is reading a book, and my father is listening to music.  My sister
Patty is riding her bicycle, and my brother Tom is skateboarding.
     My grandparents aren't in the park today.  They're at home.  My
grandmother is baking, and my grandfather is planting flowers
in the yard.
     How's  the weather in New York today?  Is it snowing?  What are
you and your family doing?
```

Answer these questions in complete sentences.

1. Where is Bob's new home? _____ It's in Los Angeles. _____

2. How's the weather in Los Angeles? _____

3. What's the temperature? _____

4. Where are Bob and his family today? _____

5. What's Bob's mother doing? _____

6. What's his father doing? _____

7. Who is Patty? _____

8. What's she doing? _____

9. Who is Tom? _____

10. What's he doing? _____

11. Are Bob's grandparents in the park? _____

12. Where are they? _____

13. What's his grandmother doing? _____

14. What's his grandfather doing? _____

15. Is Alex in Los Angeles? _____

16. Where is he? _____

F **GRAMMARRAP:** *No. She's in Spain.*

Listen. Then clap and practice.

A.	What's Jack	doing?
B.	He's working in	Rome.
A.	What's BOB	doing?
B.	He's working at	HOME.

A.	What's Jane	doing?
B.	She's working in	Spain.
A.	What's MARY	doing?
B.	She's working in	MAINE.

A.	Is Jack at	home?
B.	No. HE'S in	ROME.
A.	Is BOB in	Rome?
B.	No. HE'S at	HOME.

A.	Is Jane in	Maine?
B.	No. SHE'S in	SPAIN.
A.	Is Mary in	Spain?
B.	No. SHE'S in	MAINE.

All.	Jack's in	Rome.
	Jack's in	Rome.
	What's BOB	doing?
	He's working at	HOME.

All.	Jane's in	Spain.
	Jane's in	Spain.
	What's MARY	doing?
	She's working in	MAINE.

Activity Workbook   **39**

✓ CHECK-UP TEST: Chapters 4-6

A. Circle the correct answers.

Ex. Jack is sitting on his [computer / TV / (bicycle)] .

1. He's my [nephew / wife / sister] .

2. We're standing [on / at / in] front of our house.

3. They're swimming at the [yard / kitchen / beach] .

4. He's feeding the dog [its / it's / he] dinner.

5. He's sleeping [at / on / in] the sofa.

6. Mrs. Kent is [raining / feeding / reading] in the park.

7. We're [fixing / snowing / riding] our car.

8. They're [painting / eating / brushing] their teeth.

B. Fill in the blanks.

Ex. ___What's___ his name?

1. _____ are they? They're in Tahiti.

2. My mother's mother is my _____.

3. My sister's daughter is my _____.

4. _____ is he? He's my cousin.

5. Mr. Jones is playing a game on _____ computer.

6. My children are doing _____ homework.

7. Ms. Kim is busy. She's fixing _____ sink.

C. Write a sentence with the opposite adjective.

Ex. Their car isn't cheap. ___It's expensive.___

1. My brother isn't heavy. _____

2. They aren't short. _____

3. My computer isn't old. _____

D. Write the question.

Ex. ___Is it ugly?___ No, it isn't. It's beautiful.

1. _____ No, I'm not. I'm single.

2. _____ No, she isn't. She's old.

3. _____ No, they aren't. They're noisy.

E. Listen and choose the correct response.

Ex. No, he isn't. (a.) He's young. b. He's thin.

1. No, it isn't. a. It's difficult. b. It's small.
2. No, she isn't. a. She's rich. b. She's short.
3. No, it isn't. a. It's easy. b. It's cloudy.
4. No, he isn't. a. He's tall. b. He's loud.

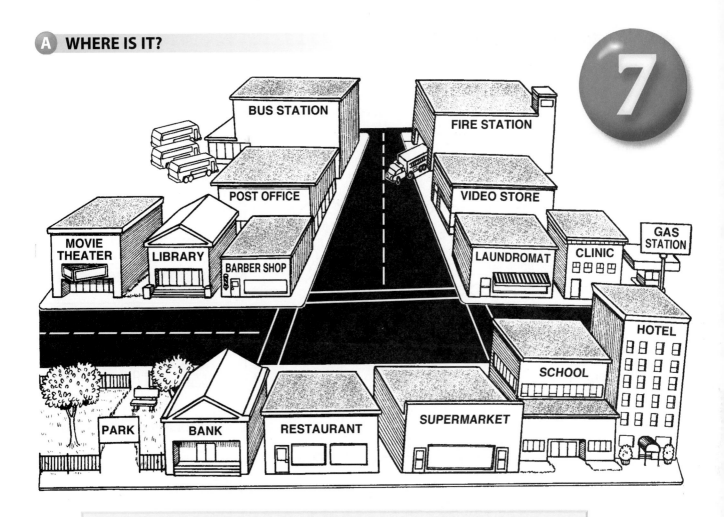

| across from | around the corner from | next to | between |

1. The bank is _____next to_____ the restaurant.

2. The bus station is _____ the fire station.

3. The library is _____ the movie theater and the barber shop.

4. The laundromat is _____ the video store.

5. The laundromat is _____ the clinic.

6. The clinic is _____ the laundromat and the gas station.

7. The clinic and the gas station are _____ the hotel.

8. The barber shop is _____ the post office.

9. The restaurant is _____ the supermarket.

10. The school is _____ the supermarket and the hotel.

11. The school is _____ the laundromat.

B WHAT ARE THEY SAYING?

Is there	There's	across from	around the corner from
there		between	next to

1. Excuse me. Is there a bank in this neighborhood?

   Yes, there is. <u>There's</u> a bank on Park Street, <u>next to</u> the school.

2. Excuse me. _____ a video store in this neighborhood?

   Yes, there is. _____ a video store on Main Street, _____ the clinic.

3. Excuse me. Is there a supermarket in this neighborhood?

   Yes, _____ is. _____ a supermarket on School Street, _____ the post office.

4. Excuse me. _____ a park in this neighborhood?

   Yes, there is. _____ a park on State Street, _____ the drug store and the library.

5. Excuse me. _____ a gas station in this neighborhood?

   Yes, _____ is. _____ a gas station on _____ Avenue, _____ the fire station.

Listen to the sentences about the buildings on the map. After each sentence, write the name on the correct building.

1. bakery	4. library	7. hair salon	10. park
2. school	5. hospital	8. supermarket	11. health club
3. department store	6. police station	9. video store	12. train station

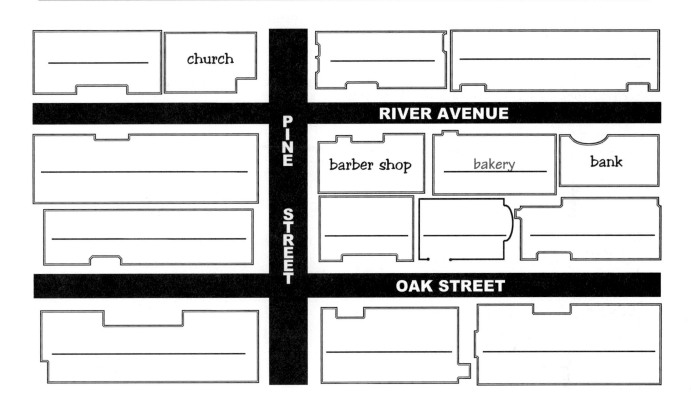

D YES OR NO?

Look at the map and answer the questions.

1. Is there a fire station on Oak Street?   Yes, there is.   (No, there isn't.)

2. Is there a hair salon across from the barber shop?   Yes, there is.   No, there isn't.

3. Is there a supermarket around the corner from the bank?   Yes, there is.   No, there isn't.

4. Is there a police station next to the hospital?   Yes, there is.   No, there isn't.

5. Is there a department store across from the school?   Yes, there is.   No, there isn't.

6. Is there a drug store on Oak Street?   Yes, there is.   No, there isn't.

7. Is there a laundromat next to the park?   Yes, there is.   No, there isn't.

8. Is there a church on River Avenue?   Yes, there is.   No, there isn't.

9. Is there a bank between the barber shop and the bakery?   Yes, there is.   No, there isn't.

GrammarRap: *Just Around the Corner*

Listen. Then clap and practice.

All. There's a nice big   supermarket   just around the   corner.

There's a good cheap   restaurant   just around the   corner.

There's a nice clean   laundromat   just around the   corner.

There's a quiet little   park   just around the   corner.

Just around the   corner?   Thanks   very much.

A. Is there a nice big   supermarket   anywhere   around here?

B. Yes, there   is.   Yes, there   is.

There's a nice big   supermarket   just around the   corner.

A. Just around the   corner?   Thanks very   much.

A. Is there a good cheap   restaurant   anywhere   around here?

B. Yes, there   is.   Yes, there   is.

There's a good cheap   restaurant   just around the   corner.

A. Just around the   corner?   Thanks very   much.

A. Is there a nice clean   laundromat   anywhere   around here?

B. Yes, there   is.   Yes, there   is.

There's a nice clean   laundromat   just around the   corner.

A. Just around the   corner?   Thanks very   much.

A. Is there a quiet little   park   anywhere   around here?

B. Yes, there   is.   Yes, there   is.

There's a quiet little   park   just around the   corner.

A. Just around the   corner?   Thanks very   much.

F WHAT ARE THEY SAYING?

is there	there is	there isn't	there are
are there	there's		there aren't

1. __Is__ __there__ an elevator in the building?

2. Yes, _____ _____.

3. How many closets _____ _____ in the apartment?

4. _____ a large closet in the bedroom, and _____ _____ two small closets in the living room.

5. _____ _____ a jacuzzi in the bathroom?

6. No, _____ _____. But _____ _____ two air conditioners in the apartment.

7. _____ _____ any washing machines in the building?

8. No, _____ _____. But _____ a laundromat across the street.

9. How many windows _____ _____ in the apartment?

10. _____ _____ three windows in the living room, and _____ one window in the bedroom.

G OUR APARTMENT BUILDING

broken	closets	escape	machines	satellite dish	mice
cats	dogs	hole	mailbox	refrigerator	stop

1. There aren't any washing _____machines_____ in the basement.

2. There's a _____ window in the bathroom.

3. There are _____ in the basement.

4. There isn't a fire _____.

5. There's a _____ in the wall in the living room.

6. There's a _____ on the roof.

7. There's a _____ in the kitchen.

8. There are two _____ in the bedroom.

9. There aren't any _____ in the building, but there are _____.

10. There isn't a bus _____ outside the building, but there's a _____.

| Yes, there is.   No, there isn't. | Yes, there are.   No, there aren't. |

1. Is there a computer in Jane's living room?

   _____ Yes, there is. _____

2. Is there a desk in the living room?

   _____

3. Are there any flowers in the living room?

   _____

4. Is there a newspaper on the table?

   _____

5. Are there any photographs on the table?

   _____

6. Are there any clothes in the closet?

   _____

7. Are there any windows in the living room?

   _____

8. Is there a cat in the living room?

   _____

9. Are there any chairs in front of the windows?

   _____

10. Is there a bookshelf in the living room?

   _____

11. Is there a cell phone next to the computer?

   _____

12. Is there a television next to the bookshelf?

   _____

13. Are there any books on the sofa?

   _____

14. Is there a guitar on the chair?

   _____

1 LOOKING FOR AN APARTMENT

a/c. = air conditioner	beaut. = beautiful	frpl(s). = fireplace(s)	nr. = near
apt. = apartment	bldg. = building	kit. = kitchen	rm(s). = room(s)
bath(s). = bathroom(s)	dinrm. = dining room	lge. = large	schl. = school
bdrm(s). = bedroom(s)	elev. = elevator	livrm. = living room	

www.UShomes.com **CHICAGO**

Quiet, sunny apt., kit., livrm., bdrm., bath., 2 frpls., no children, $900. 800-874-5555.

1. The apartment is in ____Chicago____.

2. It's quiet and _____.

3. There's a kitchen, a living room, a _____, and a _____.

4. There are two _____ in the apartment.

5. There aren't any _____ in the building.

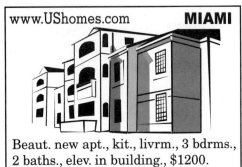

www.UShomes.com **MIAMI**

Beaut. new apt., kit., livrm., 3 bdrms., 2 baths., elev. in building., $1200. 800-874-5555.

6. The apartment is in _____.

7. It's _____ and new.

8. There are three _____ in the apartment.

9. There are _____ bathrooms.

10. There's an _____ in the building.

www.UShomes.com **NEW YORK**

Sunny, lge. apt., kit., livrm., bdrm., bath., 2 a/c., nr. schl. $1800. 800-874-5555.

11. The apartment is in _____.

12. It's sunny and _____.

13. There's a kitchen, a _____, a bedroom, and a bathroom.

14. There are two _____.

15. The apartment is near a _____.

www.UShomes.com **DALLAS**

Lge. quiet apt., kit., livrm., dinrm., 2 bdrms., 2 baths., elev. in bldg., nr. bus. $850. 800-874-5555.

16. The apartment is in _____.

17. It's large and _____.

18. There's a _____, a kitchen, and a living room.

19. There's an elevator in the _____.

20. The apartment is _____ a bus stop.

Listen. Then clap and practice.

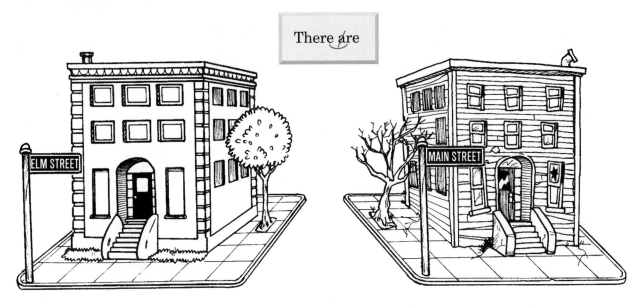

A.   Tell me about the apartment on   Elm Street.

B.   It's nice, but it   isn't very   cheap.

There's a brand new   stove in the   kitchen.

There's a beautiful   carpet on the   floor.

There are three large   windows in the   living room.

And the bedroom has a   sliding glass   door.

All.   The bedroom has a   sliding glass   door?!

B.   Yes, the bedroom has a   sliding glass   door.

A.   Tell me about the apartment on   Main Street.

B.   It's cheap, but it   isn't very   nice.

There isn't a   tub in the   bathroom.

There aren't any   lights in the   hall.

There's a broken   window in the   dining room.

And there are ten big   holes in the   wall!

All.   There are ten big   holes in the   wall?!

B.   Yes, there are ten big   holes in the   wall.

A WHAT'S THE WORD?

belt	briefcase	glasses	jeans	purse	sock	tie
blouse	coat	glove	mitten	shirt	stocking	umbrella
boots	dress	hat	necklace	shoe	suit	watch
bracelet	earring	jacket	pants	skirt	sweater	

1. _____tie_____   6. _____   11. _____

2. _____   7. _____   12. _____

3. _____   8. _____   13. _____

4. _____   9. _____   14. _____

5. _____   10. _____   15. _____

16. _____   20. _____   24. _____

17. _____   21. _____   25. _____

18. _____   22. _____   26. _____

19. _____   23. _____   27. _____

B A OR AN?

1. __a__ bus station
2. __an__ umbrella
3. _____ school
4. _____ office
5. _____ radio
6. _____ earring

7. _____ hospital
8. _____ antenna
9. _____ e-mail
10. _____ yard
11. _____ library
12. _____ cell phone

13. _____ exercise
14. _____ house
15. _____ bank
16. _____ woman
17. _____ apartment
18. _____ laundromat

19. _____ uncle
20. _____ attic
21. _____ flower
22. _____ aunt
23. _____ fax
24. _____ hotel

C SINGULAR/PLURAL

1. ____a hat____   hats
2. _____   basements
3. a dress   _____
4. a boss   _____
5. an exercise   _____
6. _____   watches
7. _____   gloves
8. a sock   _____
9. a drum   _____

10. _____   rooms
11. an earring   _____
12. _____   purses
13. a niece   _____
14. a woman   _____
15. _____   children
16. a mouse   _____
17. _____   teeth
18. _____   people

D LISTENING

Listen and circle the word you hear.

1. umbrella   (umbrellas)
2. blouse   blouses
3. coat   coats
4. computer   computers
5. shoe   shoes
6. exercise   exercises
7. dress   dresses
8. restaurant   restaurants

9. necklace   necklaces
10. earring   earrings
11. belt   belts
12. watch   watches
13. niece   nieces
14. nephew   nephews
15. shirt   shirts
16. tie   ties

LISTENING

Listen and circle the color you hear.

1. (blue)   black   3. gray   gold   5. purple   yellow

2. red   green   4. pink   silver   6. orange   brown

F **COLORS**

Write sentences about yourself, using colors.

black	gray	pink	silver
blue	green	purple	white
brown	orange	red	yellow
gold			

1. My house/apartment is. . . . .

2. My bedroom is . . . .

3. My kitchen is . . . .

4. My bathroom is . . . .

5. My living room is . . . .

6. My classroom is . . . .

7. My English book is . . . .

8. My pencils are . . . .

9. My notebook is . . . .

10. My desk is . . . .

11. My shirt/blouse is. . . . .

12. My watch is . . . .

13. My socks/stockings are . . . .

14. My coat is . . . .

15. My hat is . . . .

16. My jeans are . . . .

17. My shoes are . . . .

18. My . . . . (is/are) . . . .

19. My . . . . (is/are) . . . .

20. My . . . . (is/are) . . . .

21. My . . . . (is/are) . . . .

22. My . . . . (is/are) . . . .

23. My . . . . (is/are) . . . .

24. My . . . . (is/are) . . . .

G WHAT ARE THEY LOOKING FOR?

1. Yes, please. I'm looking for

_____ a pair of pants _____ .

2. Yes, please. I'm looking for

_____ .

3. Yes, please. I'm looking for

_____ .

4. Yes, please. I'm looking for

_____ .

5. Yes, please. I'm looking for

_____ .

6. Yes, please. I'm looking for

_____ .

7. Yes, please. I'm looking for

_____ .

8. Yes, please. I'm looking for

_____ .

9. Yes, please. I'm looking for

_____ .

Activity Workbook 53

LISTENING

Listen and put a check (✓) under the correct picture.

1. _____   2. _____   _____

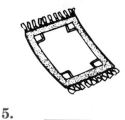  

3. _____   _____   4. _____   _____

5. _____   _____   6. _____   _____

7. _____   _____   8. _____   _____

I **LISTENING**

Listen and circle the correct word to complete the sentence.

1. ⓘ(is) red.
   are

2. is easy.
   are

3. is large.
   are

4. is gold.
   are

5. is beautiful.
   are

6. is new.
   are

7. is expensive.
   are

8. is small.
   are

9. is big.
   are

J THIS /THAT /THESE /THOSE

 this / these   that / those

  orange   yellow

1. _____This hat is orange._____   2. _____That hat is yellow._____

  brown    black

3. _____   4. _____

  expensive   cheap

5. _____   6. _____

  small    large

7. _____   8. _____

  pretty     ugly

9. _____   10. _____

  gold   silver

11. _____   12. _____

Activity Workbook   55

K SINGULAR → PLURAL

Write the sentence in the plural.

1. That coat is blue.   _Those coats are blue._

2. This bracelet is new.   _____

3. That watch is beautiful.   _____

4. This is Tom's jacket.   _____

5. This isn't your shoe.   _____

6. Is that your earring?   _____

7. That isn't your notebook.   _____

8. This person isn't rich.   _____

L PLURAL → SINGULAR

Write the sentence in the singular.

1. These sweaters are pretty.   _This sweater is pretty._

2. Those purses are expensive.   _____

3. Are these your neighbors?   _____

4. Are those your dresses?   _____

5. Those are Bill's shirts.   _____

6. These women are my friends.   _____

7. These aren't my gloves.   _____

8. Those are her cats.   _____

M SCRAMBLED SENTENCES

Unscramble the sentences. Begin each sentence with a capital letter.

1. _____I think that's my jacket._____
   jacket I that's think my

2. _____
   my these gloves new are

3. _____
   boots aren't those black your

4. _____
   year blue very this suits popular are

5. _____
   of here's nice sunglasses pair a

6. _____
   old that's car brother's my

N GRAMMARRAP: *Clothes In My Closet*

Listen. Then clap and practice.

This shirt is	red.		Old	red	shirt!	
That skirt is	blue.		New	blue	skirt!	
This shirt is	old.		Old	red	shirt!	
That skirt is	new.		New	blue	skirt!	

These suits are	silver.		New	silver	suits!	
Those boots are	gold.		Old	gold	boots!	
These suits are	new.		New	silver	suits!	
Those boots are	old.		Old	gold	boots!	

O GRAMMARRAP: *Black Leather Jacket*

Listen. Then clap and practice.

Blue	jeans,	gray	pants,	
Black	leather	jacket!		
Blue	jeans,	gray	pants,	
Black	leather	jacket!		

White	shirt,	silver	boots,	
Black	leather	jacket!		
White	shirt,	silver	boots,	
Black	leather	jacket!		

Cool	blue	jeans!		
Nice	gray	pants!		
White	shirt,	silver	boots,	
Black	leather	jacket!		

Activity Workbook   57

P THIS/ THAT/ THESE/ THOSE

| this
these | | that
those |

1. _____This_____ is my favorite pair of jeans.

_____ are my new sweaters, and

_____ is my new coat.

2. _____That_____ 's a pretty coat.

Are _____ your new boots?

3. _____ is my classroom.

_____ is the bulletin board, and

_____ are the computers.

4. Are _____ your books, and

is _____ your pencil?

5. _____ is my favorite photograph.

_____ is my mother, and

_____ are my sisters and
brothers.

6. Are _____ your cousins?

Who's _____ handsome man?

Listen and fill in the words to the song. Then listen again and sing along.

hat	those	shirt	suits	that	are	skirt	that's	boots	these	this

Is ____this___ ¹ your sweater?

Is _____ ² your _____ ³?

_____ ⁴ my blue jacket.

That's my pink _____ ⁵.

I think _____ ⁶ is my new _____ ⁷.

We're looking for _____ ⁸ and _____ ⁹.

We're washing all our clothes at the laundromat.

_____ ¹⁰ and that. At the laundromat.

This and _____ ¹¹. At the laundromat.

_____ ¹² and _____ ¹³. At the laundromat.

Are _____ ¹⁴ your mittens?

_____ ¹⁵ these your _____ ¹⁶?

_____ ¹⁷ are my socks.

Those are my bathing _____ ¹⁸.

Where _____ ¹⁹ my pantyhose?

We're looking for _____ ²⁰ and _____ ²¹.

We're washing all our clothes at the laundromat.

_____ ²² and _____ ²³.

Washing all our clothes.

_____ ²⁴ and _____ ²⁵.

At the laundromat. At the laundromat.

(Hey! Give me _____ ²⁶!)

At the laundromat!

✓ **CHECK-UP TEST: Chapters 7-8**

A. Circle the correct answers.

Ex.   My favorite color is ⟨blue⟩ .
broken ~ blue ~ big

1.   Are
these
this
that
your children?

2.   Here's a nice pair
to
on
of
stockings.

3.
Are there
Is there
There
a jacuzzi in the apartment?

4.   There's an
earring
sweater
umbrellas
on the table.

5.
Who
What
How
many windows are there
in the living room?

6.   There aren't any
man
people
hole
in the room.

7.   Dresses are over
there
their
they're
.

8.   Is there a stove in the kitchen?

No, there aren't.
No, they isn't.
No, there isn't.

B. Answer the questions.

Ex.   Where's the book store?

It's next to the bank.

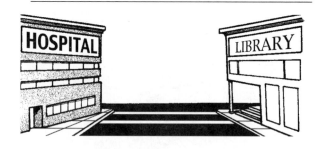

1.   Where's the bakery?

_____

2.   Where's the hospital?

_____

3.   Where's the video store?

_____

60   **Activity Workbook**

C. Circle the word that doesn't belong.

Ex.	cotton	wool	vinyl	(cheap)
1.	this	those	their	these
2.	orange	striped	gray	pink
3.	closet	bakery	hotel	school
4.	boots	necklace	shoes	socks

D. Write sentences with *this*, *that*, *these*, and *those*.

old

Ex. _____This car is old._____

large

1. _____

broken

2. _____

black

3. _____

E. Write these sentences in the plural.

Ex. That house is large.

_____*Those houses are large.*_____

1. This room is small.

_____

2. That isn't my pencil.

_____

3. Is this your boot?

_____

F. Listen and circle the correct word to complete the sentence.

Ex. 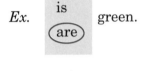 green.

1.  old.

2. is / are nice.

3. is / are beautiful.

4. is / are expensive.

Activity Workbook **61**

Correlation Key

Student Book Pages	Activity Workbook Pages	Student Book Pages	Activity Workbook Pages
Chapter 1		**Chapter 6**	
2	2–4 Exercises A–D	46–48	35–39
4–5	4–5 Exercises E–H	**Check-Up Test**	40
Chapter 2		**Chapter 7**	
8–9	6	56	41
10–11	7	57	42
12	8–9	58	43–44
14	10–11	59–60	45
16	12	61–62	46–49
Chapter 3		**Chapter 8**	
18–19	13	68–69	50–51
20–21	14–17	70	52
24	18–19	71	53
Check-Up Test	20	73	54–56
Chapter 4		74	57–59
28	21	**Check-Up Test**	60–61
29–30	22–25		
31	26		
Chapter 5			
36–37	27		
38–39	28–31		
40	32–33		
41	34		